Mindset Reset
for
Real Estate Success

*How to become #1 in your market
while enjoying a balanced life*

Orly Steinberg
"Only Orly"

Acknowledgements

"We must be willing to let go of the life we have planned so as to have the life that is waiting for us."

—E. M Forrester

I have so much gratitude for my full, rewarding life, and the many people who have supported me on my journey.

First and foremost, I am grateful for my life partner, Aharon, who made me feel like my life truly began when we became one. I would not be who I am today without his love and support.

I have been fortunate to work with so many mentors who have helped me transform my life, and who continue to inspire me today. They include, but are not limited to: Eleanor Lockard, Howard Brinton, Leslie McDonnell, Debbie Yost, Dr. Fred Grosse, and of course, my dear mother, Yaffa.

I am eternally grateful to my team, who allow me to forge ahead, remain true to who I am, and soar in new directions: Noreen Sherry, Carol Conger, Diana Fili, Beth Herina, Jill Harrington, and my first admin, Cathy Hartwick, who has been with me since 1993. I would also like to thank my dear friend, Paula Clark, for being one of my staunchest supporters since we met, and for always having my back.

My three amazing daughters—Tara, Monica, and Jaymee—are my true legacy. I am so proud of the women they are today. I appreciate all the joy, encouragement, and support they add to my life.

I am grateful to my yoga teacher and friend, Cheryl Kiviat, for giving me the tools that keep me sane and grounded, and feed my body and soul.

Last but not least, I'm grateful for Sue Klein, my editor, who heard and understood my voice, and helped me convey my mindset reset for real estate, and life, success to you.

How to use this Book:
Again and Again

"Our self-image and our habits tend to go together. Change one and you will automatically change the other."

—Dr. Maxwell Maltz

People often ask me: "How did you brand yourself? How did you build so much market share? How did you build your team? How do you travel so much? How did you raise three young daughters while growing your career?"

I want to say: "It's a long story." Now I can say: "Read my book. And then let's talk."

I wrote this book to help women, in particular, with tools for advancing their careers and approaching real estate more like a business while retaining life balance, as much as that is possible.

This book is about my journey, and the many lessons I have learned along the way. The tools I share with you are by no means overnight, quick fixes. There is a lot of information in these pages. It took years of reading, going to conferences, and emulating successful people to learn what is possible if you alter your mindset, set goals, and do the work to obtain them. It took more than three years to gather my thoughts, write them down, and glean the pearls of wisdom I now impart to you.

Some sections will resonate with you now, and some will make more sense later. I recommend reading the book from cover to cover first, taking notes, and highlighting things that stand out and speak to you. Take a break after each segment to reflect, answer the questions, and gain your own clarity. Return to relevant chapters when you need them.

One of my mentors, Howard Brinton, taught me: "When there is a lesson to be learned, a teacher will appear." Some of the lessons you will encounter the first time you read this may not resonate with you at first. However, as you progress along your journey, you may find yourself searching for some of the tools within this book when you are ready to implement them.

Take a moment to download a "Wheel of Life" at www.mindsetresetforrealestatesuccess.com, and fill it out in order to identify the areas of your life that are most important to you, so you can start developing plans to achieve your goals. You may want to revisit, and revise, your wheel often as you progress. Your goals and priorities will evolve. Plan on it.

I hope you use this book like a workbook: dog ear it, write in it, and keep it close by. Think of it as a handy reference you can turn to at various stages of your own journey.

Contents

Forward.. 11

Chapter 1: Life Lessons in Resilience 13
Balancing Cultures — the Beginning *13*
Turning Knowledge into Power — Making it Work...................... *15*
Keeping Family in Balance.. *16*
What Does Support Look Like for You?...................................... *19*
Chapter 2: Discovering Yourself; Life by Design 21
Defining Your Success.. *23*
Giving Back *26*
Chapter 3: Gaining Clarity; the Pursuit of 'Why' 27
Focus on Why *28*
Clarify Core Values.. *28*
What is Your Why?.. *30*
Identify an "I Have to…"... *31*
Define Your "I have to…"... *32*
Next: Address the "How".. *33*
Be Authentic *33*
Sustain Connections.. *34*
What About Your Relationships? *36*
Pursue Success Your Way.. *37*
Define Success.. *39*
Chapter 4: Starting Your Day Right 42
Making Your Heart Sing.. *43*
Perpetually Grateful.. *44*
Setting Intentions and Affirmations: 5 Pillars............................ *45*
Affirming Your 5 Pillars.. *48*

Chapter 5: Identifying Your Pillars; Tracking Goals 49
Plot Your Wheel *50*
Create Your Own Wheel of Life *52*
Striking a Balance; Adjusting as You Go *53*
Reassessing and Setting New Goals *54*
Chapter 6: Digging Deeper; Making Your 5 Pillars Work for You 59
Pillar One: Health *60*
How do you stay healthy? *61*
Thriving Under Adversity; it's a Choice *63*
Accept Help; Rely on Your People *64*
Pillar Two: Personal Relationships *65*
Pillar Three: Personal Growth *68*
Pillar Four: Business *70*
Pillar Five: Wealth *71*
Chapter 7: Money Funds Your Life; Work to Make What You Need 73
Tracking Real Estate Income and Expenses *74*
In the Beginning. *75*
Realizing a Return on Your Investment *75*
Money Matters; What Matters to You? *76*
Money is a Life Force; How does it Drive You? *77*
Money Memories *78*
How do You Perceive Money? *81*
Money Measurements *82*
Dollars and Sense *83*
Chapter 8: Achieving Financial Freedom; How Much is Enough? 84
Financial Security *85*
Calculate Your Costs *86*
Financial Vitality *87*
The Extras *88*
Financial Independence *88*
Financial Freedom *89*
Financial Freedom Goals *90*
Life Happens *91*
Money Lessons *92*
Dig Deep *95*

Chapter 9: Mentors, Coaches, and Building Teams...........**101**
Accessing Star Power... *102*
Seizing Opportunity.. *105*
Choosing the Right People for the Right Jobs............................... *106*
The Four Personality Types: D-I-S-C.. *108*
Next Level Team Building... *111*

Chapter 10: Building a Business Foundation; Putting Systems in Place **113**
Finding the Right Replacement... *115*

Chapter 11: Running Your Business like a Business; And it is a Business **118**
Generate Leads... *119*
Decide When to Build a Team... *125*

Chapter 12: Conquering FOMO; Keeping it Real.............. **127**
Conference Prep *129*
Follow Your Agenda; Implement What Works for You *130*
Re-Evaluate Your "Have to"; Re-invent Your Why..................... *131*
Checking In.. *133*
Control Your Calendar; Before it Controls You *134*

Chapter 13: Facing Real Estate Challenges; Mindset Matters **136**
Overcoming Challenges 101: Listen *137*
Tell the Truth; Manage Your Time *137*
Deals Will Go South; Be Prepared... *138*
Know When to Let Go... *140*
Keeping it Together... *141*
Be a Consultant, Not a Social Worker....................................... *142*
Get Ahead of Ghosting.. *144*
Make Time for You *145*
Set Boundaries... *146*
Make the Most of Your Time... *147*

Chapter 14: Make Things Happen; Focus on Your Strengths **148**
Anchor Your Vision *149*
Adapt Your Attitude... *150*

Chapter 15: Attitude is Contagious; Make Yours Worth Catching 152

Making Choices *153*

Defining Abundance and Scarcity; A Real-life Comparison *154*

Chapter 16: Adapting through Crisis; And Crises Will Happen 156

Embrace Change *157*

Prepare for the Next Crisis *159*

Emerge Stronger *160*

Who Do You Choose to Be in a Crisis? *162*

Financial Adversity — And the importance of your Credit Score *163*

What Does Your Credit Score Say About You? *165*

Chapter 17: Living the Legacy; Charting Your Future 166

Chapter 18: In Conclusion; Baby Steps… 168

My Reading List 171

About the Author 177

Forward

Finding balance takes work. It's a moving target.

Picture a gymnast walking on a balance beam. She shifts her outstretched arms up or down on each side, focusing on her next step, and adjusting accordingly to keep moving forward.

I found real estate at 30. I was living in an unfamiliar area with a newborn and a two-year-old. My husband was busy building a travel agency business in New York City. Through trial and error, constant learning, absorbing, communicating, focusing, and adjusting my balance, I grew to become the number one realtor in my town and one of the top one percent in the United States. All this while raising three daughters, traveling around the world, practicing yoga, nurturing friendships, being active in my community, and enjoying regular date nights with my husband.

This book is about the journey: both mine and yours. Real estate changed my life and helped me define the person I want to be. As I wanted more, I learned that life can be enriched with less. I went from feeling like I was running a marathon from the minute I opened my eyes in the morning to starting my days with relaxed intention. My days are now joyful, productive, fun, and abundant.

My clients and my community know me as "Only Orly." My guiding principles for accomplishing everything you set out to do without losing yourself in the process can work for you, too.

This is a book you will want to keep by your bedside to ground you, calm you, motivate you, and inspire you to be the person you want to be. Work through the exercises to gain clarity and develop a clear vision of your dreams. Discover habits, systems, and mindsets that will guide you throughout your personal and professional life, no matter what is going on. Revisit to track, monitor, and re-adjust. Because that's how balance works.

Enjoy the journey!

Chapter 1
Life Lessons in Resilience

It wasn't always easy, and at times I didn't know how I got through the day. I was barely 30, with a newborn and a two-year-old, while embarking on a brand new career in real estate.

I knew nothing about real estate or Ringwood, the town I now lived and worked in. My first day at the office, my manager and first mentor, Eleanor Lockard, suggested I preview some of the homes for sale in "Stonetown." Stonetown? "Where is Stonetown?" I asked. I had a lot to learn.

BALANCING CULTURES — THE BEGINNING

I had no idea how much I had to learn. I grew up in New York City. As a teenager, I spent summers and weekends at our lakefront vacation home in Ringwood, New Jersey. I knew little else about New Jersey, or the neighborhoods, like Stonetown, within my new, rural enclave.

I was born in the Washington Heights neighborhood of Manhattan. When I was two months old, my parents moved back to Israel with me and my two-year-old brother, Joey.

My mother is a fifth generation Israeli, and my father is a first generation American, whose parents were pre-WWII Polish immigrants. I was raised bilingually, and biculturally, in Israel until I was six. My father worked as a freelance cameraman for various news organizations. He made good money as a freelancer working on the prolonged trial of Adolf Eichmann, the first Holocaust war criminal to be caught and tried for his atrocities. When the trial was over, my parents sold their car and used their savings to go to the states for a year.

We returned to Washington Heights in September 1963. Two months later, President John F. Kennedy was assassinated. My father found himself in demand, covering many news stories about this monumental event. This catapulted his career, which prompted us to stay in the United States.

I was used to walking over sand dunes to go to kindergarten in Israel, a small country the size of New Jersey. Now I had to cross a busy six-lane intersection over Broadway to get to first grade. A crossing guard helped my eight-year-old brother and me get there safely.

Being in a huge, new school, which was the size of a city block, was very overwhelming. I got lost going to the bathroom that first day. Eventually, I learned to love, and thrive in, this new environment.

I learned to believe in myself. If my mother believed I could cross Broadway to get to school at six years old, then I believed I could do it, too.

We moved to the suburbs of Kew Garden Hills, Queens, when I was 10. At 14, I took the bus to the subway to go back into the city to attend the High School of Art and Design. After high school, I went to the City College of New York in Harlem, where I majored in film production, trying to follow in my father's footsteps.

By then, I was a city girl, through and through. Years later, when I moved to Ringwood, I would say, "I live in New York, I just sleep in New Jersey." I knew nothing about New Jersey, very little about my town, and I had to learn how to sell real estate in the suburbs. Fortunately, I'm a great student.

TURNING KNOWLEDGE INTO POWER — MAKING IT WORK

I was always the nerd who actually liked school and doing book reports. School gave me opportunities to grow. Even as a young girl, I appreciated how the best teachers opened my eyes, and my mind, to new ideas, thoughts and concepts. I'm grateful I gained this insight so early in my life. Learning remains a passion that continues to propel me through my life and career.

I pursued education on a fast track—graduating from college magna cum laude in three years. I was eager to learn all that I could and start my life. That was when I first began to understand how "Knowledge is power." The more you learn, the better you can be.

This is how I approached my career in real estate. I wanted to learn everything I could. I took advantage of every learning opportunity and seminar I could find. I sat in the front row, took notes, and figured out what I could implement immediately. In the office, I listened to top agents talking on the phone for hours, and emulated their dialogue with clients.

While pursuing this professional development, I paid a babysitter to watch my two daughters, Tara and Monica. Even though I only earned $7,000 my first year it was $7,000 more than I had before. It was a start. And in 1987, $20,000 was considered a good, average salary. I was on my way.

Working made me feel productive. It helped me keep my sanity. I realized I was not well suited to be a stay-at-home mom. It can be hard for mothers to admit this. It's not for everyone. I tried it for about two years with Tara, and frankly, I was bored.

I needed something more to keep me engaged in life. So I gave myself permission to not be a stay-at-home mother. Real estate gave me the flexibility to start off working six hours a day until my business took off. It allowed me to ease back into work until the girls were older.

In 1988, I paid a sitter six dollars an hour. This was money I couldn't afford to waste. I had to make every minute, and every dollar, count. During work hours, I kept busy making calls, setting appointments, taking people to see homes, and developing my marketing and my brand.

I was determined to make this work. If I was going to be a realtor, I was going to be a business woman, too. I set out to learn everything I needed to know to run my business like a business, which is something most realtors still don't realize they need to do.

I opened a business bank account, and deposited 25% of every commission check like I was paying myself a referral fee. This way, I could feel comfortable investing this money into my business without having to tap into the joint account I share with my husband, Aharon.

KEEPING FAMILY IN BALANCE

I couldn't have built my career, or my business, without my husband's loving support. I know that not all realtors have the benefit of a built-in support network. Many single parents must juggle the challenges of family life and a real estate career on their own. Being able to rely on a spouse, or parents, can be a huge game changer.

Aharon is a travel agent who runs his own agency. We are both self-employed, which can be both a positive and a negative. There are many positives: flexibility; opportunities for growth; control over our own earning potential; and having the ability to grow our teams and shape our own culture. However, neither one of us has the security of a paycheck or benefits.

We are both super attentive to running and building our businesses. We understand the challenges, and the time we need to commit to clients at all hours.

It can be difficult for a spouse with a salaried position, and a more regular schedule, to understand the demands of an entrepreneurial business. In the early days, Aharon left the house at 6 a.m. and didn't get home until 9 p.m. When the girls were young, I was essentially a single parent Monday-Friday. I would jokingly assure him that even though he saw us in our pajamas both when he left the house early, and when he came home late, we really did get dressed, go to work and school, and have a productive day in between.

Commuting from Ringwood, NJ, to Manhattan takes about an hour and a half. It makes for a long day. Clearly, during the week, I was on my own.

I had a list of babysitters to call when I had afternoon and evening appointments. Keep in mind, in the late 80s and 90s, we did not have computers and cell phones. If a client called the land line and needed to see a house, or wanted to list their house, I had to juggle things and find a babysitter the old fashioned way in order to run out the door.

I scrambled to make sure the girls got to their sports events, had dinner, and did their homework. I was blessed to have sweet, well-behaved daughters who understood this was their "norm". I told them that if I worked hard and met my goals, we could all go on a great family vacation together. I needed them to understand, and buy into my goals, so they wouldn't be upset when I had to leave.

And then there were the weekends, which are the busiest time for a realtor. That's when most people are available. Booking appointments is always the first priority. I started booking appointments on Tuesday, so that by Friday I knew what my weekend would look like. I made sure I had four to five appointments on Saturday, and one or two appointments on Sunday, including an Open House.

Every Saturday morning, I wrote down tasks for Aharon. I left him laundry, shopping lists, and schedules for birthday parties and sports events.

That's where teamwork helped most. I loved knowing that on Saturday mornings all I had to do was get myself ready and go to work. I didn't have to juggle getting the girls ready for school, coordinating car pools, preparing lunches and breakfast, picking them up from school, supervising homework, driving them to sports or dance practice, preparing dinner, and working. On Saturdays and Sundays, I worked. It was nice to be able to focus on just one thing. I even enjoyed doing Open Houses where I could quietly read a book if no one came in.

Aharon allowed me to focus completely on my clients, with little distraction on the weekends. He also supported me when I went away to conferences, and never complained about the extra house work he picked up while I was gone. I was also fortunate that my parents were close by to help with the girls during the week whenever I was away.

I was a woman on a mission, and I knew where I wanted to go; however, I needed help. It is challenging, if not impossible, to succeed as a realtor and manage a family without a supportive spouse.

Who supports you?

_____

_____

_____

_____

Who could you reach out to when you need a support system?

_____

_____

_____

_____

WHAT DOES SUPPORT LOOK LIKE FOR YOU?

A healthy, balanced marriage is rarely 50/50. Some days it is 60/40. Other days it is 90/10. It varies, depending on what is more important to each person.

Aharon and I have always worked at maintaining a true partnership. For example, we do the laundry like a team relay race. One of us starts a load in the washing machine, while the other transfers it to the dryer, depending on who is home when it's done. Either one, or both of us, will fold the laundry and put it away. The rule is: once we start the laundry it has to be finished and put away that day. There is nothing I hate more than laundry sitting in the wet cycle or getting wrinkled in the dryer. This is a healthy, balanced partnership.

Another thing I hated was spending Sundays taking out clients, doing an Open House, and getting home exhausted at 6 p.m. only to hear: "What's for dinner?" I would get so frustrated and upset.

Ultimately, I sat down with Aharon and told him how much I hated those three words. We came to an agreement: he could order dinner, cook it, or buy ingredients for me to cook, as long as he decided what dinner would be. That straightforward communication worked. From then on, he did a great job managing dinner on Sunday nights.

I know many women can relate to this. They have felt my pain. But how many women actually let their spouses know what is not working for them?

The key is to know what is really bothering you, and to communicate that effectively to another person along with a potential solution. This sure beats feeling resentful and angry. Believe me, I have felt resentful and angry, too; however, I realize it's up to me to initiate change.

What issues could you address with your spouse to make your partnership stronger?

_____

_____

_____

_____

_____

_____

_____

Chapter 2
Discovering Yourself; Life by Design

After graduating college in three years with a film and television degree, I moved to Israel for a year. I got a job at the ABC News Tel Aviv bureau, and lived with a roommate in my parents' three-bedroom house. I also met an Israeli soldier who was a photographer in the Israeli army, fell in love, and got engaged. I was 21. That's a lot for one year at any age, but that's how I roll.

Everything was going well, until we got into a heated argument about something really stupid. Up until then, we were in the honeymoon phase. This was our first, and ultimately last fight; but it caused me to pause and re-evaluate our engagement. My intuition told me to break it off and come back home to New York City.

I didn't really know who I was. How could I? I was so young, and still had much to learn. Recording my thoughts in a journal during this transitional, pivotal, point in my life, helped me realize I needed to discover who I was before I could merge my life with anyone else.

I needed to find out what I liked, and what I didn't like, about the world around me. So I went to movies by myself, bought different clothes, read a lot of books, and listened to different types of music.

After eight months of focusing completely on myself, I concluded that I was now ready to meet someone new. My journal served as a record of that progression—something I could refer back to as a way to trace my journey and plot my future.

I'm telling you this story because, even at a young age, I intuitively knew I needed to gain clarity. I had to take the time to understand what my needs were, and what I wanted from life, in order to pursue my goals.

You can either design your life, or life will just happen to you. I prefer to be proactive, rather than reactive. First, you need to know, and understand, yourself. Stop and take the time to ask yourself questions that will help you discover who you are on a deeper level. This will help you visualize what success might look like for you.

DEFINING YOUR SUCCESS

What do you love to do for fun?

_____

_____

_____

What do you need to thrive?

_____

_____

_____

When do you sparkle — that feeling you get when everything in your life is going so well you suddenly feel like giggling?

_____

_____

_____

Consider your answers to the questions above in order to define what success is for you.

_____

_____

_____

Now, consider the bigger picture. How do you see yourself in the world? We are all influenced by our environment, society, television, and our peers, who tell us about their definitions of success.

How do you think others see you? The house you live in, the car you drive, the clothes you wear, and even your zip code can define who you are to some people. Do these things define success for you? Do they reveal who you are at a core level? They might, and I make no judgement if they do.

I define success as being free to be your own person. To me, success is being able to choose what you want to do on any given day, while maintaining a comfortable income stream, spending time with people you really enjoy, and nurturing a sense of inner joy and peace. To me, success is feeling whole: knowing you are at the exact right place, at the right time, doing what you are supposed to be doing.

What fulfills you? Are you truly present enough to notice, and enjoy, all the wonderful things in your life: flowers blooming, birds chirping, meaningful conversations with good friends, delicious meals, and feeling good in your own body?

It's easy to get caught up in the fear of missing out (FOMO). There is nothing wrong with wanting nice things, as long as they don't define you. I believe the people you surround yourself with help define you, too. Think about what really matters to you. I have had the privilege of surrounding myself with the most amazing human beings who bring me up, inspire me, and motivate me to be the best I can be.

Recently, I was asked to be a speaker on a panel of realtors who talked about business planning. One component focused on giving back to the community. Two amazing women shared how they incorporated philanthropy into their businesses.

One realtor buys shower trucks for the homeless that give them a place to clean up and get clean underwear. She also hires army wives from around the country to be virtual assistants, so they can work from wherever they are stationed. Another realtor started renting all the musical instruments for the children in her school district. Because of her sponsorship, there is still a music program in her community.

I have met so many successful people who follow their passions by giving back to charities that are important to them. I have been involved with several charities, including the Center for Food Action (CFA), and am still searching for that one cause that really speaks to me.

GIVING BACK

What causes, or issues, are you passionate about?

_____

_____

_____

Who could benefit from your guidance or assistance?

_____

_____

_____

How can you help? Could you volunteer with an existing program, or even come up with a new solution to address an emerging need?

_____

_____

_____

Helping others helps put our own lives into perspective. My mother always taught me that it is better to be on the side of being able to give than having to receive. What can you give to help someone else?

Chapter 3
Gaining Clarity; the Pursuit of 'Why'

"Success comes when we wake up every day in the never ending pursuit of WHY we do WHAT we do. Our achievements, WHAT we do, serve as the milestones to indicate we are on the right path. We need both."

—Simon Sinek

What does success mean for you? For me, it is the ability to truly live my life by design and be financially free.

How have I designed my life? I arrange my time every week so that I can take three yoga classes, go on at least six listing appointments, pick up my grandchildren twice, and enjoy a date night with Aharon.

I also set aside the time and money to travel throughout the world four times a year. I go to conferences that enlighten me and allow me to grow. And I take comfort in knowing I can do, or buy, just about anything I want and not have to worry because I have created enough passive income to sustain my lifestyle.

Focus on Why

Having a clear vision prevents you from getting distracted and spending time on things that don't serve your dreams and aspirations. You'll be able to focus on things that bring you closer to your life goals.

It is so easy to get side tracked. As long as you keep your "Whys" and each corresponding "I have to" front and center, they will help you refocus on your goals.

Life throws challenges and obstacles at us every day. What we do with them, and how we handle them, makes the difference between success and failure. We can skirt around an issue, work through it, or leap over it. The goal is to overcome obstacles in the best way possible. It's even better when we learn a lesson or two along the way.

Clarify Core Values

I wasn't born into my current lifestyle. I created it over time, as I evolved and learned from those around me. While the values that guide you may shift over time, it's important to maintain a consistent central core, or theme. Knowing what your core values are is crucial for living your life authentically.

My core values are:

- Stability
- Joy
- Family
- Love
- Growth
- Awareness

What is your motivation for getting up each morning?

Is it that you have to, or is it because you can't wait to start the day? My mother-in-law used to say: "A person needs a reason to get up in the morning, and a reason to be tired at night."

WHAT IS YOUR WHY?

What are your core values?

_____

_____

_____

_____

What drives you?

_____

_____

_____

_____

What are your passions, both personally and professionally?

_____

_____

_____

Where do you see yourself 5 and 10 years from now?

_____

_____

_____

WHAT IS YOUR WHY? (CONTINUED)

Are you motivated by money? How much is enough?

_____

_____

_____

Are you motivated by success or ego?

_____

_____

_____

IDENTIFY AN "I HAVE TO..."

We all have at least one "I have to..." For example, I realized early in my marriage that I wanted a certain lifestyle, and in order to achieve it I had to earn some serious money.

It wasn't about wanting a lot of material things. We needed a larger home if we were going to expand our family from two to three daughters. We also wanted to send the girls to private Jewish school for their formative years, and travel to Israel every two years to familiarize them with their roots and develop relationships with their family there. Our financial "I have to…" was grounded in our core values of family, comfort, and stability.

DEFINE YOUR "I HAVE TO..."

What do you have to do to live the life you want?

_____

_____

_____

_____

_____

_____

Is what you're doing now, in your career and/or your personal life, giving you pleasure?

_____

_____

_____

_____

Are you passionate about what you're doing?

_____

_____

_____

_____

Next: Address the "How"

When I began my career at 30, with a two-year-old and a newborn, I would ask myself: What is the epitome of a successful realtor? What does she look like? How does she dress? What does she sound like on the phone? What dialogues and scripts does she use?

Then I set out to create an image of a "professional realtor." Most, if not all, of my clients didn't even know I was married with young children. That was by choice. I just wanted them to think of me as their realtor.

I was too insecure to let people know I had a family. I worked so hard to build my professional image that I lost some of my humanity. As I became more successful, that hyper focus made me seem less approachable to some people. I decided I needed to work on that.

Be Authentic

As I became more secure in my success, I started to soften up and allow the public to see me as their neighbor and friend, with similar interests. It was OK to be their realtor, and a wife and mother with children. I became more authentic and vulnerable, relatable and approachable.

This was harder to do before the days of Facebook. Now social media allows me to share my authentic self in front of more people, and my business continues to soar.

Today, I am on the other end of that spectrum. One day, I was babysitting my grandchildren—Jack, who is four, and Maya, who is 20 months—at their house. I normally don't take calls while I'm with them, but this time I did. It was a new buyer asking questions about a new listing I had just launched. While we were on the phone, Jack opened the front door and Maya started walking out with him. I managed to pull them back in and lock the door as they screamed in protest.

I apologized and told the buyer I was babysitting my grandchildren. He laughed, and was very understanding while we finished our conversation. I would never have had the confidence to be that authentic in my early days. The more relaxed version of me ended up converting him as a buyer and we sold him a house.

SUSTAIN CONNECTIONS

As I started to sell more and more houses, I realized I had a gift for connecting with people. I had a talent for making them feel comfortable, and guiding them through major life decisions about their finances, such as choosing the right home to reflect their lifestyle and needs.

I learned early on that being a realtor is not about brick and mortar. It's about meeting people and building relationships. I love counseling people, and finding out what makes them tick. I enjoy spending hours with families and observing how they interact. I learn so much. I take home lessons about what not to do with my own family, as well as wonderful ideas for enhancing our lives.

I remember being called to list the homes of people who were getting divorced right after their kids left for college, and wondering why they came to that conclusion after doing all the hard work of raising their family. It seemed to me that the hard work was behind them. Their lives should get easier now. Unfortunately, I still see this pattern a lot, and can understand it a little better now that I, too, am an empty nester.

As our lives evolve and change, sometimes people move in different directions, and develop different interests and priorities. In order to avoid this, I made sure Aharon and I went out every Saturday night, and went away together at least once a year. Going somewhere local for a weekend counts, too.

I was fortunate to have parents close by to watch the girls. I remember telling Aharon I would always love him, but I wanted to make sure we still liked each other after the girls left home. Thankfully, we still both love, and like, each other—which is equally, if not more, important.

WHAT ABOUT YOUR RELATIONSHIPS?

How are your relationships with your spouse and children? Really?

_____

_____

_____

Do you enjoy spending time with your spouse alone? How did you survive the COVID-19 quarantine?

_____

_____

_____

Who would you choose to quarantine with? And what might that look like?

_____

_____

_____

_____

Relationships aren't always easy. They can be a lot of work. I constantly have to focus on maintaining, and enhancing, my relationships. I try to concentrate on who needs more nurturing, or attention, at any given time. It could be one of my daughters, my parents, Aharon, or a dear friend. It's always shifting.

PURSUE SUCCESS YOUR WAY

The meaning of success is different for everyone. A farmer gets joy out of reaping the harvest, and the rewards of a healthy crop. A mom appreciates when her children eat their vegetables at dinner and go to bed without incident. We are not all looking for—nor do we want—the same things.

Not everyone wants fame and fortune. It's easy to get swept up in society's idea of success, and the material trappings that come with it. Sure, we all want more money, but does your net worth truly measure your success? Very often that is the message we see and hear.

We have been programmed to pay more respect to someone with an impressive title and a six to seven figure salary. However, a happy-go-lucky street musician who lands a gig playing for a paying audience, no matter the fee, may see their accomplishment as equally successful.

When I was eight, I loved to wake up early and sit for hours coloring and drawing. I basked in the freedom of doing what gave me joy. As an adult, I am working on achieving that sense of freedom again, with no self-judgement about what I could, or should, be doing.

When you pursue success through achievements, and you view your achievements as your final destination, it can be hard to feel satisfied, no matter how big your bank account gets.

For me, success comes from deeply connecting with people every day. I value learning from others. I am fortunate to be able to offer people wisdom, or some comfort, during trying times. My job involves guiding people who are often at a crossroad, and helping them make good decisions to move on to a better place. I can be objective. I can do my best to help, and show homeowners that I truly have their best interests at heart, not just my own.

I also enjoy the thrill of winning someone over for a new listing, and successfully negotiating contracts. My earnings are simply a measurement—a financial guideline—for success. What are your guidelines for success?

DEFINE SUCCESS

I ask you again to define what success means to you, and only you.

_____

_____

_____

What is your driving purpose, cause, or belief?

_____

_____

_____

What has to happen in order for you to become a success?

_____

_____

_____

What struggles, or sacrifices, would you be willing to tolerate to achieve success?

_____

_____

_____

_____

DEFINE SUCCESS (CONTINUED)

What did your eight-year-old self love to do?

_____

_____

_____

What things do you do in the course of your career today that bring you joy?

_____

_____

_____

Identify something you do now that you would like to change?

_____

_____

_____

If you could wave a magic wand, and money was no object, what would you do?

_____

_____

_____

_____

I will ask some of these questions several times throughout the book, because I feel it is vital for you to know yourself and what drives you. As you start to think about different aspects of your life, you may re-evaluate some of your answers. And that's OK. In fact, it's healthy. It's what keeps life fresh and vital.

I encourage you to revisit what you write here periodically to make sure you are staying on track and shifting where needed in order to move forward.

Chapter 4
Starting Your Day Right

How do you start your day?

I used to wake up with a start as if someone was setting off a starter pistol at the beginning of a race: open eyes, brush teeth, shower, get dressed, get the girls up, prepare them for school, eat breakfast, drive to school, and get to work before 8:30 am. Rinse and repeat the next day. There is nothing unusual about that kind of morning for millions of people.

Over the years I discovered there might be a better way to start my day. It often begins the night before, thinking about what is on my plate. Am I over booked? Will everyone, including me, be able to get what they need? Will I be able to accomplish what I set out to do? Will it get me closer to my goals?

There is a difference between need and want. We all have obligations: those are the things we tend to focus on first. But what about the things we really want to do? Before you know it, the day is over and you didn't get that "me time" you were hoping for to do something for yourself or just simply have some fun.

Other people pull us in different directions, asking us to help them, and it's hard to say "No". Just remember, when you say "Yes" to one thing, you are saying "No" to something else. Very often, that ends up being ourselves. Before you know it, you are lying in bed asking yourself, "Where did the day go?"

MAKING YOUR HEART SING

When I think ahead about the next day, I try to incorporate the things that make my heart sing, as well as actions that bring me closer to my goals. For example, I can plan to make prospecting calls for two hours—with a goal of getting three listing appointments—and then plan an hour massage. Once something is in my schedule, I rarely deviate from it.

Getting up early gives me time to ground myself. Using the principles of the "Miracle Morning" by Hal Elrod, I set out to start my day with a positive attitude. I begin with a light morning workout, or a little yoga—something that gets my body moving and circulates oxygen in my blood. Depending on my mood, and what time it is, within 30 minutes of waking up I either do 45 minutes on the treadmill or a 10-minute stretch.

I drink a tall glass of water with my supplements, and I spend 10-15 minutes writing 10 things I am grateful for. It could be the birds singing outside my window, a tree blossoming after a long and cold winter, my first cup of coffee, a productive day booking listing appointments, fun times with friends, or a good night's sleep, which so many people take for granted. I always conclude by acknowledging my gratefulness for the same six things: our home, our love, our family, our friends, our health, and our wealth.

PERPETUALLY GRATEFUL

- I am grateful for spending time with Aharon just sitting on the couch, holding hands, and watching TV.

- I am grateful for fun dinners with friends, laughing and enjoying each other's company.

- I am grateful for my health, not being in any pain, and being warm on a winter's day.

- I am grateful for a great home cooked meal at my mother's house, and for still having my parents, who are in their late 80s, in my life.

- I am grateful when my grandchildren call my name and hug me.

It feels good to know that simple things, such as looking at my garden and enjoying a clean, happy home, can make me happy and complete.

Expressing my gratitude in this way creates a mental check list of all the things that are important to me, big and small, and I recognize how blessed I am.

I invite you to start your own daily gratitude journal. It's amazing how taking five-10 minutes every day to actually write down what you're grateful for can ground you for the day ahead.

SETTING INTENTIONS AND AFFIRMATIONS: 5 PILLARS

After I complete my gratitude list, I set aside another five-10 minutes to write out my intentions and affirmations for the day and share them with three groups of women I call my support sisters. These women are also realtors. One group is my team. One group is agents I coach. The other group is made up of dear friends who are also top agents around the country.

I visualize each person as I add her name to an email, which helps me to start visualizing the day ahead and all of its potential. My intentions incorporate my "5 pillars," which encompass important aspects of my life.

My first exposure to the 5 Pillars concept was at a business conference full of realtors led by Dr. Fred Grosse, Debbie Yost and Patrick Lilly. It was the first conference I attended where we didn't discuss how to sell more houses. The mindset exercises I learned there taught me how to live more deeply, and delve further below the surface to take care of myself inside and out.

You cannot achieve balance without consistently incorporating everything that matters into your life. It is impossible to maintain perfect balance in all aspects of your life all the time. The practice of identifying your top priorities, your 5 Pillars, helps you stay mindful of what matters most. Then, on any given day, you can decide which area of your life needs the most attention.

My 5 Pillars are:

1. Health
2. Wealth
3. Personal Growth
4. Business
5. Relationships

My daily intentions and affirmations might look something like this:

- *Pillar:* Health

    o *Intention:* reminding myself to do the things that keep me healthy, such as making good eating choices, doing yoga, and getting exercise.

    o *Affirmation*—I am nurturing my body and soul at yoga today, and making good eating choices to take care of my future body.

- *Pillar:* Business Goals

    o *Intention:* staying focused on what I need to do today to bring me closer to my business goals.

    o *Affirmation*—I am able to effortlessly attract three new "come list me" calls and buyers who love working with me and my team as we create more raving fans with our amazing skills and service.

- *Pillar:* Wealth

    o *Intention:* conscientiously doing things that will contribute to my wealth building goals.

- o *Affirmation*—I am paying off my debt and investing in my future, confident in my ability to thrive and plan for my financial security.

- *Pillar:* Personal Relationships

  - o *Intention:* thinking about the people in my life I care about. I may focus on supporting a friend who needs healing prayers or connecting with someone for fun. I'm always thinking about my family.

  - o *Affirmation*—I am sending healing energy to ____. I am having fun this evening with _____. I am deeply connecting with _____. I am looking forward to enjoying a date night with Aharon.

- *Pillar:* Personal Growth

  - o *Intention:* It is important for me to grow and evolve as a person and challenge myself.

  - o *Affirmation*—I am enjoying the world around me, and am open to meeting new and interesting people.

I end my affirmations with:

I am always surrounded by joy, love and abundance, living my life by design.

AFFIRMING YOUR 5 PILLARS

Write one affirmation and one intention for each of these 5 Pillars:

• Health:

_____

_____

• Business:

_____

_____

• Wealth:

_____

_____

• Personal Relationships:

_____

_____

• Personal Growth:

_____

_____

Chapter 5
Identifying Your Pillars; Tracking Goals

Focusing on my 5 Pillars helps me develop goals for the week, month and year. In order to stay on course, I need to dig deeper and hold myself accountable. Fortunately there is a tool for that, too.

Creating a Wheel of Life helps me gain clarity. It helps me visualize where I am right now in each of my 5 pillars so I can work on advancing to where I'd like to be. You can find a template for creating your own wheel at www.mindsetresetforrealestatesuccess.com.

PLOT YOUR WHEEL

Your wheel could look something like the one below, and contain up to eight segments. Here are some suggested pillars:

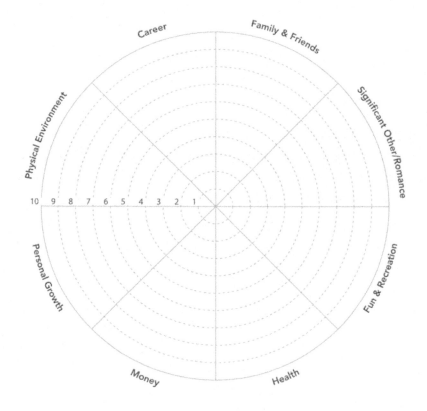

The premise is simple and powerful. Draw a segment for each of your 5 Pillars. Then, starting from the middle of the circle, fill in how far you've come toward achieving your goals in each area of your life, on a scale of 1-10. This helps you see what you need to pay attention to first.

You can also make a separate wheel for each of your five pillars. Or you can isolate just one pillar that seems to be more of a challenge. Your dedicated wheels might look something like this:

HEALTH

Your health wheel could be divided into sections that address weight goals, exercise, healthy eating, drinking water, doctor appointments, meditation, etc.

WEALTH

A wealth wheel might include debt reduction, savings (how much), income (be specific), investments, and wealth building.

RELATIONSHIPS

You can expand your relationships wheel to include your spouse/life partner, friends, children, parents, siblings, co-workers, or anyone else who has an impact on your life.

BUSINESS

Segment the business wheel to address your goals for income, education, systems, team building, skills training, prospecting, or whatever else you'd like to address.

PERSONAL GROWTH

Your personal growth pillar may change frequently, depending on your current interests. This wheel might include reading books, recreation, travel, lectures/learning, conferences, retreats, new friendships, creativity, and mindfulness.

Once you drill down within each of these areas, and decide where you would like to improve your life, you can set measurable goals and develop an action plan.

Next comes the fun part: you can start designing your life one piece at a time.

CREATE YOUR OWN WHEEL OF LIFE

What five areas of your life would you love to develop?

1. _____

2. _____

3. _____

4. _____

5. _____

You can download a blank Wheel of Life on my website: www.mindsetresetforrealestatesuccess.com. Assign one of your 5 Pillars to each triangle, and start filling it in.

The key is to be completely honest with yourself. No one is watching or judging you. This is just for you. Isolate an area you want to start working on first, and make a list of all the things you can do to start growing and improving.

STRIKING A BALANCE; ADJUSTING AS YOU GO

I like to start each year with self-reflection, thinking about the 5 Pillars that are most important to me. I ask myself:

- What are my goals for each pillar?

- Where do I stand at this moment in my life?

Then I write my vision for the year ahead, including all the things I would like to accomplish. This isn't a New Year's resolution. I prefer to formulate a plan, instead of a short-lived wish list.

REASSESSING AND SETTING NEW GOALS

Look ahead to the end of this year. Imagine that you have just experienced your best year ever because you have met or exceeded your goals. Think big. You've lost weight, you look fabulous, and you have more energy. You've met your business goals and increased revenue so that you can invest in your future. You finally took that trip to Disney World with your family.

How does that feel?

_____

_____

Now ask yourself:

• How would I feel if I hadn't accomplished my goals?

_____

_____

• Who would I be disappointing? Myself? My family? My clients? My employees?

_____

_____

• What actions do I need to take to ensure I achieve my best year ever?

_____

_____

REASSESSING AND SETTING NEW GOALS
(CONTINUED)

Look at your career, for example:

• **Where are you working now?**

_____

_____

• **How much do you earn?**

_____

_____

• **How much do you need to earn to achieve your goals?**

_____

_____

• **What action steps are you willing to take in order to accomplish this?**

_____

_____

   Daily:

_____

_____

REASSESSING AND SETTING NEW GOALS
(CONTINUED)

Weekly:

_____

_____

Monthly:

_____

_____

• Why is this important to you?

_____

_____

Let's explore your whys:

• Why is it important for you to take your income to the next level?

_____

_____

_____

• Why do you want to be the best realtor in your area?

_____

_____

REASSESSING AND SETTING NEW GOALS
(CONTINUED)

• **What would that look like? Feel like?**

_____

_____

_____

Go deep into your heart and explore why this is so important to you:

• **Do you want to get out of financial debt?**

_____

_____

• **Do you want to buy a house? A larger house? For whom?**

_____

_____

• **Do you want to have more money for a better car? Are you dreaming of a fantasy family vacation? Do you need college tuition for you or for your children? Be specific.**

_____

_____

_____

Put a picture of your "why" in front of you and look at it every day. Look at it when you're feeling frustrated.

Better yet, move it every day. Touch it. We tend to become oblivious to things that are always there. We might glance at them occasionally. However, if you touch and move your picture frequently, you will start engaging with your "why" on a regular basis.

Chapter 6
Digging Deeper; Making Your 5 Pillars Work for You

Because my 5 Pillars have become such a guidepost for me, they are naturally integrated into my life. At the end of each year, I spend several hours reviewing them to make sure they're still relevant. This is a good time to make the adjustments I need to move forward.

I like to say: "If you don't evolve you dissolve." That's how the singer, Usher, describes his career path: "If you don't evolve, you dissolve. You evolve or you evaporate." Constant change is the only way to keep developing your talents. This fits my philosophy, too.

A stagnant body of water becomes polluted with algae and other contaminants. A moving, breathing, and flowing river stays clean and vibrant. It's mesmerizing to watch as the water rushes by. It's the same for us. Personal growth is essential until the day we die.

Each month, I spend an hour or so thinking and planning the specific projects and goals I need to work on within each of my 5 pillars. This could be as specific as making an appointment with my dentist for my health, or making a financial investment to increase my wealth.

On Sunday nights, I like to spend about 30 minutes planning the week ahead. I might book appointments on my business calendar, plan a date night for my relationship pillar, or schedule yoga and/or a massage for my health pillar.

My daily five-10 minute morning ritual of setting intentions and affirmations also aligns with my 5 Pillars. I try to be as specific as possible, so I can feel a sense of accomplishment at the end of the day.

Let's break it down further:

PILLAR ONE: HEALTH

I am not a fitness fanatic. I'm not athletic. If you are, you are one step ahead of me. However, I do make sure to move my body every day and make good eating choices. I practice yoga three times a week, and walk on my treadmill five days a week.

I eat three times a day, with a healthy snack or two in between. Raw almonds or vegetables are two of my favorite go-to energy boosters. I often have eggs or avocado toast for breakfast; sushi, salad or yogurt for lunch; and enjoy a healthy, balanced dinner with a salad, protein, carb and a vegetable. Anyone who knows me knows I am also a sugar addict; however, I try to limit chocolate and dessert.

This is how I choose to take care of my body. What is your approach to living a healthy life, with room for a few guilty pleasures? Once you start thinking about this, the list will grow, or at least you'll be motivated to make it grow!

HOW DO YOU STAY HEALTHY?

How/what I eat:

_____

_____

_____

_____

_____

Indulgences:

_____

_____

_____

_____

_____

Setting Limits:

_____

_____

_____

_____

_____

How do you stay healthy?
(Continued)

Exercise:

_____

_____

_____

_____

_____

Self-care:

_____

_____

_____

_____

_____

Other:

_____

_____

_____

_____

_____

THRIVING UNDER ADVERSITY; IT'S A CHOICE

I try to schedule most of my annual doctor visits during my birthday month as a gift to myself for longevity. In fact, during one of those November visits in 2009, after having a routine mammogram, I discovered I had breast cancer. This took me on a year-long journey full of appointments and procedures, including a double mastectomy. I also benefitted from many life lessons and blessings.

My first lesson, after receiving my diagnosis from a very condescending breast surgeon, was to find someone who would give me the care and attention I deserve. I became my own best advocate, interviewing three more breast surgeons until I found the right one. I let these doctors know I was not just there for a second opinion. I was looking for the right person to take me on this journey, which I hoped would be a short one.

Dr. McIntosh was the only surgeon who insisted I do a breast MRI. Everyone else thought a simple lumpectomy and radiation would do the trick. The MRI revealed a third nodule, which led to a mastectomy. I opted to do both breasts, as I like a matching pair, and didn't want to go through this ordeal again. I didn't want to take the 25% chance that cancer could develop in the other breast.

I was in the office with my team close by when Dr. McIntosh called with the MRI results at 10 am. Everyone was quiet while I listened to her on the phone. I asked her about the next steps, and she recommended I see a plastic surgeon to discuss reconstruction options.

Next lesson: take action and stay in control (as much as you can). By 1 pm that day, my friend, Ruth, and I were already consulting with a plastic surgeon. So many people become paralyzed in the face of bad news, don't take action, and don't ask for the support they need. My philosophy is to be proactive, no matter what.

We decided on a double mastectomy and Tram Flap reconstruction surgery. It took seven hours. Tram Flap surgery uses your stomach muscle to reconstruct your breast, so that you avoid anything artificial. The seven-week recovery is difficult and painful. It's not for everyone. In fact, surgeons no longer do this procedure. There are now alternative options, so do your research.

ACCEPT HELP; RELY ON YOUR PEOPLE

My team took over the business for two months during my recovery. Because we had good systems in place, everything ran smoothly. In fact, they sold 16 houses in the first month alone.

Aharon worked from home, caring for me in the most loving and nurturing way. My daughters helped, too. They would crawl into bed with me to watch movies and keep me company. Friends visited with food and flowers.

Another lesson: sometimes you have to let go and let others care for you. I loved receiving get well cards from all over the country. I grew stronger by letting myself be vulnerable instead of stoic. This bolsters others as well.

Allowing someone to be there for you in a time of need is one of the biggest compliments you can give. It lets them know you trust them, and are letting them in to help you. Realtor friends from other companies even offered to run my business for me. And my dear friend, Leslie McDonnell, flew in for two days from Chicago.

It sounds strange, but my experience beating breast cancer, with the help of friends and family, was one of the most wonderful events of my life. Attitude is key in everything you do in life, and my attitude was fabulous. I discovered how many people love me and are there for me. I discovered my own strength and my own vulnerability. I learned how to depend on others, which has always been difficult for me.

I gained so much from my experiences that I even wrote a blog to help other women in similar situations called "onlyorlybeatsbreastcancer .com".

PILLAR TWO: PERSONAL RELATIONSHIPS

Personal relationships—having a close knit, loving family and dear friends—is one of my most cherished core values. It's everything to me. My supportive husband, three beautiful, independent, daughters, two brothers, parents, and several close, special friendships sustain me and give me so much joy.

My relationship with Aharon grounds me. I like to say I am like a kite soaring high up in the sky, swaying in the wind from the occasional turbulence of life and nature, and Aharon is my constant. He holds on to the kite string to make sure I stay grounded and safe. Always.

It would be impossible for me to sustain a successful career, and a full life, without my supportive spouse. Aharon picks up the slack, helps with the laundry, shares errands, and pays the bills. He helped raise our children. He rubs my back at night, enabling me to let go and finally relax after a challenging day. Do you have someone in your life who supports you this way?

I've always believed relationships are rarely, if ever, a 50/50 proposition; however, they should always equal 100%. On some days, one person may need more attention, making the equation 90/10. A decision, such as picking a movie or a restaurant, may be more important to one person, making the ratio 70/30.

Sometimes the ratio shifts in the middle of a project. When Aharon and I decided to renovate our master bathroom, I kept busy designing it, working with the contractor, and choosing most of the tiles, fixtures and paint colors. Aharon didn't seem to mind, or care, about me making these choices.

Towards the end of the project, I had to go to a business conference for a few days and Aharon took over. He wanted a certain kind of toilet, which was important to him. That was the one thing I didn't care about. He chose it while I was away, and I was fine with that. We both got what was important to us, so it was a happy 90/10 experience.

Since then, we have renovated two more bathrooms. Aharon is now more interested in having more input in decorating decisions, and we've enjoyed going out together to pick out and buy tiles and fixtures we both love. This is a great example of how our relationship has evolved.

This is how balance works. Things don't always have to be equal in order to be balanced, as long as both sides are happy. I cannot say this enough: it takes effort and focus to sustain relationships; however, the work shouldn't be too hard. It should be a labor of love, so to speak.

My family and friends are always on my mind and in my heart. I try to set aside time with them all, and enjoy planning special "dates" with my husband, daughters, parents and friends.

Favorite activities include: painting and wine class parties; mother/daughter high teas; Broadway shows, concerts and comedy nights; walking food tours; and brunches in New York City with our mother/daughter friends.

We love to shop. Taking my mother to all of her specialty food stores so she can cook for us — and everyone else she knows — is always a pleasure. In the summer, we enjoy hiking and spending time around the pool. We also love to entertain family and friends. In fact, my daughter Monica's friends call our house the Steinberg Resort.

One of my dreams—high up on my bucket list—was to be able to take my husband, daughters, their husbands and significant boyfriends, and my grandchildren on a fabulous family vacation every year. I am happy to say this has become a reality.

We have treated everyone to an annual trip since 2008, and will continue to do so as our family grows. We have been to Israel many times, Italy, France, Spain, and on several cruises. You don't have to be extravagant. A long weekend away to someplace within driving distance can be fabulous, too. My husband, Aharon, is a travel consultant, which helps makes our trips more affordable.

I never apologize for the life I have created for me and my family. I worked very hard for it. I earned it. In fact, when I bought my dream house in 2018 everyone said: "You deserve it!" It truly touched my heart every single time I heard those words from a friend, client, coworker, or someone in my community. The universe knew I needed to hear it and give myself permission to make the move.

The universe also gives me permission to celebrate once in a while. As long as you work hard, celebrating is truly necessary.

To me, celebrating can be about looking forward to something in the future, intensifying a present moment, or reflecting on something positive from the past. It's savoring both small and big moments in life. It could be celebrating making 10, 50, or 100 calls with a cup of coffee, or going out to a nice dinner to celebrate a big win.

I like to stop and savor every win throughout my day: setting up appointments, getting another listing, writing up an offer, successfully negotiating a sale, or settling difficult home inspection issues. Taking a moment to celebrate, and express gratitude, helps you live more in the moment, and focus on the positives.

PILLAR THREE: PERSONAL GROWTH

I'm always in growth mode. I love to read and search for lessons in books, movies and conferences. I also get a lot out of my interactions with other people.

Personal growth is a lifelong pursuit. It takes knowing yourself and knowing what you want out of life. It takes being mindful about your surroundings. It takes knowing your core values, living them, and surrounding yourself with people who share them. It takes being able to learn from your successes and failures. It takes a desire to learn from others.

One of my favorite things about being a realtor is having the privilege of meeting so many different people who come to us to list and sell their homes. We become an important part of their lives for a few months, and learn valuable lessons from their experiences.

I love listening to people's stories. What a privilege it is to get to know someone new, and learn about how they raise their children, the vacations they go on, and how they have fun, spend money, handle relationships, and decorate their homes. Listening deeply—delving deeply into the soul of what someone is saying—can reveal a lot about a person's life journey.

I look for indicators to help me understand how to relate to, and work with, someone:

- What is their pain?
- What is their fear?
- What are their stresses?
- What are their goals?

Many people fear the unknown, which can be stressful. They may be overwhelmed, which causes them pain and holds them back. Getting to the crux of someone's underlying agenda(s), by listening carefully and asking meaningful questions, builds trust and confidence. It feels good to be understood.

True salesmanship should seem effortless. It should feel more consultative. Have you ever worked with a salesperson who tells you all about the bells and whistles of a car or computer instead of trying to understand your needs? When you ask questions, and truly listen, you can better guide a client to a decision.

I recently did a market evaluation for a couple in their early 50s whose boys were away at college. When I got to the house, the wife informed me her husband was still upstairs and wasn't feeling well. I proceeded to go through the house, minus his bedroom, and consult with her about marketing and pricing. Shortly after I left, he started throwing up blood and she took him to an Emergency Room. I stayed in touch with her, and five months later she told me he passed away and she would be ready to sell the house soon.

When I went back to her home, feeling terrible about her loss, I was ready to give her all my sympathy and compassion. I was surprised to see how strong she was. She had already cleaned out his stuff and the house was ready to sell. She told me she, too, was surprised at her own inner strength.

I have seen people become paralyzed after such a loss, and leave everything exactly the way it was before the person they loved passed away. The way someone handles a situation like this is a tribute to their resiliency. I hope that when my time comes to deal with this kind of situation (many years from now) I will somehow find the strength to keep moving forward the way she did.

I love observing all kinds of relationships. I see young couples who are so excited and involved with the day-to-day tasks of child rearing, and multi-generational families who are living together for financial, and practical, reasons. I learn so much from watching all of their family dynamics.

It's so nice to see families that I sold homes to 10, 20, and 30 years ago grow. I remember when some of these children were born, and now they are graduating college, getting married and having children of their own. I've seen several clients become grandparents and retire happily. It's an honor to be a part of their journey and grow along with them.

PILLAR FOUR: BUSINESS

This pillar is the back bone for growing your business. First, you need to define your WHY, so you can set your goals. Dig deep and be clear about what you truly want. Then put together a plan to get there.

Take the time to hone your skills so that you are constantly mastering your craft. Work on listing presentations. Role play objections buyers, sellers, and "expireds" may have. Practice negotiating skills. Learn all you can about branding and marketing yourself.

Set up systems to streamline your business. Expand to the next level by tracking expenses, making sure you are earning a worthwhile return on investments (ROI), and sourcing where your business is coming from.

Figure out what is working, and what is not, so you can focus more on things that are profitable.

Decide what you need or want to focus on each day. It could be lead generation, implementing new systems, marketing and branding, taking a class to enhance your skills, or something else you've been meaning to tackle.

Clearly, we need to do all of these things to grow; however, setting a daily intention in one area at time is an effective way to accomplish your goals.

Potential daily intentions:

- I am having deep conversations with 10 past clients today.

- I am taking a webinar on creating Facebook groups in order to grow my business.

- I am meeting with my buyer's agents to go over scripting so we can sharpen our saw (skills), and work more effectively.

PILLAR FIVE: WEALTH

While this pillar may be the one people think they want the most, they tend to work on it the least. Building a business, and building wealth, should go hand in hand. From the beginning, my business mindset was to fund my life to provide the financial security I need to thrive.

The wealth pillar addresses paying off debt, and investing incrementally until you reach financial freedom. You can focus on small and large building blocks every day, and every week, to reach your goals.

Putting a big picture goal together, and breaking it down into small parts, helps you tackle wealth goals daily. Set your intentions and affirmations accordingly to help you stay focused on the prize.

Potential goals:

- I am effortlessly paying all my bills at the end of the month.

- I am investing in one rental property this year that builds my passive income wealth.

Chapter 7
Money Funds Your Life; Work to Make What You Need

This is a very personal chapter for me. I am honored to share my journey, and my evolving relationship with money, so that you can learn from my experiences.

I started my career in real estate in April 1986. I earned $7,000 my first year. Tara was 18 months old, and I had just discovered I was pregnant with Monica. I realized no one else would hire me at that point, so I had nothing to lose. Whatever I earned would be a bonus.

I also realized I was not meant to be a stay at home mom. I needed more. I needed my own identity. I needed to be productive, and achieve my own success.

I have always been an education junkie. I had nothing to lose, and everything to gain, by going to school for my real estate license. I was excited to learn a new craft, and I knew I needed to set goals to give myself direction and achieve clear objectives.

For me, making money was an "I have to." I wanted to provide a better lifestyle for my family. My first goal was to create a steady stream of business, instead of riding the roller coaster of intermittent closings most agents contend with.

First, I set out to bring in at least one closing every month. Then I strived for two closings a month, and so forth, until I earned a more substantial, steady stream of income. This took years. It also took a lot of patience and perseverance.

Another goal: buy a larger home so we could grow our family. In April 1989, we were able to buy a four bedroom colonial backing up to watershed property. We added Jaymee to our family, and raised our three daughters there for 30 years.

TRACKING REAL ESTATE INCOME AND EXPENSES

Some people think making money in real estate is easy. Wrong! It takes close to $2,500 in dues and fees just to start a real estate career. And you should have at least six months cash reserve if you don't have someone to support you.

If you are fortunate enough to have a support system, think of it as a safety net; don't rely on it. It should be there to give you a roof over your head and provide the basics while you figure things out.

Consider yourself unemployed until someone decides to hire you by signing a listing or a sales contract. This is a long-distance marathon. It's important to think about the "why" and the "I have to" that motivates you every day so you can hit the ground running and build your new career.

Remember: you are responsible for paying your own quarterly taxes, and making up any difference at the end of the year if you earn more than you thought you would. That may sound like a good problem to have; however, many realtors run into trouble when they forget to pay the IRS.

How do you figure out your quarterly taxes? After your first full year as a realtor, you will be able to set an income benchmark. Make sure to track increases, or decreases, in your quarterly earnings, and adjust payments if necessary.

IN THE BEGINNING...

How can you survive with such an inconsistent income, while you still have considerable living and marketing expenses? This is why you need a six-month cash reserve, and/or support from another source.

While you're building your business, cut down on all other expenses until you have a consistent cash flow. Being a realtor takes a lot of sacrifice. It is not for the weak at heart. You may have to have another source of income, or another job, at first.

REALIZING A RETURN ON YOUR INVESTMENT

Once your business starts to flow, start tracking your dollars. It is imperative to know what you are spending your money on so you can calculate ROI.

The goal—believe it or not—is to be 40% profitable before taxes. This is an industry standard. I have consistently achieved 72% profitability for the last several years by watching, and tracking, my expenses.

Don't get caught up in every shiny new object someone tries to sell you. Truly analyze and calculate if it is a good investment. There will always be some degree of risk. I have made my fair share of bad decisions, too. I still believe it is better to try new things than to remain stagnant.

Figure out your annual budget, and identify what you have available to spend on growth tactics. In the beginning, you will probably need to spend 25% of your profit, or more, to set your business on solid ground and start growing. Count on that.

You should get three times the return on every investment. Source every single lead so you can track where your business is coming from. Then you can put more money into what is working, and stop doing things that aren't.

Most importantly, calculate your fixed personal and professional expenses to establish a minimum earnings goal. These expenses could include rent or mortgage, food, utilities, car payments, etc.

MONEY MATTERS; WHAT MATTERS TO YOU?

As you delve deeper into finances, start exploring your core values related to money, because they will (or at least they should) drive many of your decisions. Aharon and I are driven to attain security for our family, since both of us are self-employed and have never had a steady salary or benefits. Because of this, we make sure to live within, or even under, our means. We never know what the next year may bring.

We live in a very money-driven society, where we are constantly being told what we should have, drive, and wear. It is so easy to get caught up in spending money to achieve stature according to someone else's core values. Here are some good financial habits to help you stay debt free:

1. Be mindful of your spending habits. In order to lower your debt, or pay it off entirely, you'll need to track your expenses so you can see where your money is going. Ask yourself: "Do I need it? Or do I want it?" Act accordingly.

2. Create a budget and stick with it. Calculate all your "must have" expenses and develop realistic guidelines. Include a dollar amount for paying down debts.

3. Pay off one debt at a time, starting with the one that has the highest interest rate.

4. Make it a habit to save a percentage of every commission for a "rainy day". Treat this as a line item in your budget. Putting this money away will give you the confidence, and security, you need to make it through a down market, or any other tough time.

5. Keep contributing to your retirement. If money is tight, consider temporarily reducing your contribution, and look for additional ways to make budget cuts. Set a goal to increase your retirement funding as soon as you can. If you don't take care of your future, no one else will.

MONEY IS A LIFE FORCE; HOW DOES IT DRIVE YOU?

Money has a life energy of its own, with emotional, psychological, and financial attachments. Your emotional connection to money begins as a young child. It is tied to how your parents perceived money, and how you were brought up.

MONEY MEMORIES

What was your first recollection of money?

_____

_____

_____

_____

Do you remember the first time you touched it?

_____

_____

_____

_____

Who gave it to you?

_____

_____

_____

Was it a grandparent or your parents?

_____

_____

_____

MONEY MEMORIES
(CONTINUED)

How did you perceive money, and what it could do for you?

_____

_____

_____

_____

Were you raised in a house full of abundance or scarcity—both physically and psychologically?

_____

_____

_____

_____

Fortunately, I have had a life of abundance. Whether my parents had money or not—and we did not have any in the early years—I never felt I lacked for anything.

When we lived in Israel, and my father worked freelance, we had a running tab in the grocery store. That was not unusual in those days. Even when we didn't have enough money to pay our monthly food bill, the owner never questioned us because we were American and he figured we would get it to him in due time.

When we moved to the United States, my father joined the film union and got a job with WABC News. Once we were more comfortable, we moved to a single family house in the suburbs of Queens, NY.

I remember coming home from school when I was around 10, and finding socks, underwear, and other clothes by the dozens on the steps going up to my bedroom. My mother just replenished whatever she thought I needed and left it waiting for me before I even knew I needed it. This is a pattern I grew up with.

Food was also abundant, and there were always guests filling our house with laughter. My Israeli mother loves to entertain, and to have a house full of people she can feed. The fact that she is a gourmet cook doesn't hurt.

My mother handled the money in our house, and she did it brilliantly with an eighth grade education, speaking English as a second language. She was the one who decided we should move from our two bedroom apartment in New York City to a house in Queens. She was also the driving force behind buying our lakefront weekend home in Ringwood, NJ, and the many investment properties that would become my parents' source of passive income. She was a natural business woman.

I was blessed to be born to parents who not only lived outside of the box and drew outside the lines, they didn't even know there was a box. As a news cameraman, my father never worked a 9-5 job in an office environment. Every day was different, and he loved it that way. My mother grew up in Israel in the 40s and 50s, when everything was a struggle. She had to find solutions to challenges on a daily basis. Her strong survival skills continue to serve her well today.

I grew up connecting money to emotional and psychological abundance and security. I learned how to handle money both as a tool for achieving a comfortable life now, and for investing in a secure future.

HOW DO YOU PERCEIVE MONEY?

Is money a means to an end, or are you enjoying the ride?

_____

_____

_____

Is money meant to be spent, or is it more important to save for a secure life? How can you strike a balance?

_____

_____

_____

_____

Is money a measurement of your success? How so?

_____

_____

_____

How do you handle money? Do you hold on to it too tightly? Or do you let it go too freely?

_____

_____

_____

These are all important questions to ask as you make decisions about your finances.

MONEY MEASUREMENTS

Money can be a measurement of success, ego, materialism, and power. People use it as a yardstick to compare themselves to others. We can be wealthy—even rich—compared to some people, and still feel unfulfilled because others have more.

How much is enough for you? What are your dreams? Are you fulfilling your needs and wants? Or are you just competing with someone else? The answers to these questions provide important checks and balances to keep us from getting caught up in someone else's dreams.

For me, it has always been about providing my family with a comfortable lifestyle devoid of debt. It has been about building financial stability for the future. It has never been about chasing name brands, keeping up with the Joneses, or showing off to anyone.

In order to get to the next level of your life, you need to think bigger. Aim higher—even higher than what you think is high. Aim far beyond what feels comfortable.

DOLLARS AND SENSE

Answering big questions will lead to thinking bigger. Fill in the blanks with your ideal income.

What is your annual income goal? _____

Now double it: _____

How about in three years? _____

Five years? _____

What net worth do you desire? _____

Look ahead to three years: _____

Five years? _____

Twenty 20 years/retirement? _____

Chapter 8
Achieving Financial Freedom; How Much is Enough?

In his book, "Money: Master the Game," Tony Robbins discusses seven simple steps to financial freedom. As I climb the ladder, and become more successful, I sometimes ask: How much is enough?

Robbins outlines four financial phases:

1. Financial Security
2. Financial Vitality
3. Financial Independence
4. Financial Freedom

In order to achieve true financial freedom, you need to either earn more money, or save more money, and invest the difference. If you need to alter your lifestyle to do that, think about what you can sacrifice now in order to gain financial security later.

There are many ways to invest. The key is to maximize the rate of return on your investments and create a lifetime supply of income. Find the vehicles that make the most sense for you. And start now! It is never too late.

Make an appointment with a good financial advisor who can guide you. You can accumulate a mass of wealth by investing in a portfolio of low-cost, tax-advantaged, well-allocated investment vehicles. And there are ways to convert your wealth into an annuity that will pay you a consistent stream of income every month for the rest of your life.

Imagine how you would feel if you could count on a steady stream of monthly income for life.

FINANCIAL SECURITY

What does financial security mean to you? Is it about taking care of essentials for the rest of your life: mortgage, utilities, food, transportation, and insurance? Or are you looking for more?

It is important to know how much money you will need to live a financially secure life. First, calculate the cost of your essentials per year, and set an annual income goal for now and for your retirement that will cover them. Determine your minimum requirements. You may want to add other, more variable essentials, too, such as clothes, entertainment, health, education, reading, and personal care.

Make sure to consider variables, such as the cost of living in your current and potential locations, your lifestyle, and your stage of life. You will need to recalculate and adjust periodically, taking into account your family status—whether you're single, a young couple starting a family, or are empty nesters. Always project forward to anticipate your needs for the next five, 10, and 20 years.

CALCULATE YOUR COSTS

Let's get started. It's OK to estimate. Maybe you plan on buying a new car, or you just paid off a car loan. Gas, utility, and food costs, will fluctuate, too. Do your best to get a baseline.

Essentials:

Mortgage/Rent: _____

Utilities: _____

Groceries: _____

Transportation: _____

Insurance: _____

Additional Expenses:

Clothes: _____

Personal Care: _____

Restaurants: _____

Health: _____

Exercise: _____

Education: _____

Entertainment: _____

FINANCIAL VITALITY

Once you've achieved financial security, you can start enjoying additional extras, such as better clothes, fine dining, massages, regular manicures and pedicures, more time at the hair salon, vacations, nice cars, and other luxury items.

The passive income you've established should take care of everything that falls under your "financial security" budget, so that you can work towards attaining extra income to afford more things on your "financial vitality" list.

THE EXTRAS

What extras would you like to be able to include on your financial vitality list?

Let's start with the top 10:

1. _____

2. _____

3. _____

4. _____

5. _____

6. _____

7. _____

8. _____

9. _____

10. _____

FINANCIAL INDEPENDENCE

When you reach the financial independence stage, you should have enough passive income to cover everything on both your financial security and financial vitality lists.

You no longer have to work. You work because you love what you do and you're passionate about it. Your money is now working for you; not the other way around. You are on the road to financial freedom, where you can relax, invest, and start taking more calculated growth risks.

FINANCIAL FREEDOM

"Dare to live the dreams you have dreamed for yourself."

—Ralph Waldo Emerson

When you've achieved true financial freedom, you will have everything you've ever wanted—and you won't have to work for it anymore. You will be able to enjoy significant luxuries without a financial care in the world.

FINANCIAL FREEDOM GOALS

In order to get to this stage, you have to dream really big.
Ask yourself:

• **What annual income do I need to afford everything I've ever wanted?**

_____

• **What, exactly, am I striving for: a bigger home, a vacation home, travel, a boat, or luxury cars?**

_____

_____

_____

_____

_____

• **Do I want to be philanthropic and allocate a substantial amount of money for charity? If so, how much? And where?**

_____

_____

_____

_____

_____

Set goals, and calculate exactly how much passive income you will need to get to the stage you desire. Then figure out how to get it.

Even if you never reach complete financial freedom, wouldn't it be wonderful to achieve financial vitality or independence?

LIFE HAPPENS

Real life happens while you're working on your financial goals. It won't always be easy.

Whenever adversity strikes, I ask myself: "What is the worst that could happen?" Then I think of people who are in a much worse position.

I go back to being grateful. I believe that, in the scheme of life, if you can solve a problem with money then it's not the worst challenge you could face.

For example: When my daughter, Tara, was in high school, I hired a seamstress to design and sew her prom dress. Three days before the prom, Tara burst into my room crying. She hated the dress I had made for her. And she felt bad that she didn't want to wear it to the prom.

Although this may seem like a trivial problem, I couldn't let her feel horrible on such an important occasion. This could affect her self-esteem for years. I didn't want it to be the high school memory she carried with her throughout her life.

So I told her not to worry; everything would be okay. I went to the mall the next day and bought eight dresses for her to try on during her dinner break at work. She found one she loved, and I was able to save the day. She had a wonderful time at her prom and looked beautiful.

I told her that as long as we can address a problem with money, we are fortunate. We won't be able to fix everything that way. Money can't always solve situations related to health, love, or a myriad of other things.

MONEY LESSONS

I have learned many lessons about money that I'm happy to share with you:

1. INVEST WISELY.

Knowledge is power. The more you learn, the more power you have. Education is key. Know your options. Start conservatively, with one investment at a time, and build a strong portfolio. Don't over leverage yourself all at once.

I like to buy with cash, or 50% down, so I know that no matter what the market does, I will always have equity. This also increases my annual income and profit margin, and helps build a passive income stream for retirement.

Some investors prefer to leverage their money and mortgage 80% so they can buy more investments. I prefer to be the tortoise instead of the hare. Slow and steady wins the race. Choose what works for you, and invest wisely.

2. CUT SPENDING.

Instead of giving in to all of the shiny objects you desire—such as luxury cars, expensive jewelry, or extravagant vacations—make sure to set aside funds for your future. If you spend too much money on instant gratification, you may wind up with a house of cards that could collapse on you at any time. This is a real possibility when you are self-employed and cannot rely on a steady pay check.

When the real estate market is good, and you're doing well, stockpile cash. Then, when the market shifts, you can take advantage of more investment opportunities to help you ride out a less profitable period.

3. Live below your means.

"Don't buy things you can't afford with money you don't have to impress people you don't like"

—Dave Ramsey

Living below your means is not a new concept; however, it is crucial for living a wealthy, financially secure life. In fact, it may be the most important financial lesson I taught all three of my daughters.

When each of them got their first credit cards I said: "If you have the money to pay for whatever you want at the end of the month, then go ahead and buy it. If you don't have the money now, don't buy it."

This sounds pretty simple; however, we often want instant gratification and are tempted to buy something we think will enhance our life or make us feel better, whether we have the money to pay for it or not. This can creep up on you, with more and more revolving debt, and get you in to trouble.

We live in an uncertain world. Living under your means helps you avoid financial hardship. I have listed many homes that were upside down on their mortgage because people fell on hard times and couldn't recover from their escalating debt.

Remember, when you are self-employed you wake up every morning "unemployed" until someone decides to hire you. Set up a forced savings plan. Pay yourself first, and remember to put away 33% for taxes.

4. SCHEDULE YOUR FINANCIAL FUTURE.

Schedule a day, at least once a year, to go somewhere that inspires you—a place where you can enjoy quiet time to reflect and meditate on designing your life. Take your significant other with you so you can plan your future together. I like to do this quarterly.

Block out time, and schedule everything that it is important to you. Put your big rocks—which are the most important things—in first. This could be vacations, time with family, exercise, prospecting leads, etc. Then, you can prioritize making them happen. Whatever else you can fit in is a bonus.

DIG DEEP

Ask yourself:

• **What is going great in my life?**

_____

_____

_____

• **What would I like more of?**

_____

_____

_____

• **What would I like less of?**

_____

_____

_____

Create a goal sheet and review your choices:

• **What's feeding you?**

_____

_____

_____

_____

Dig Deep (Continued)

• **What is depleting you?**

_____

_____

_____

_____

• **What would you like to happen in the following time frames?**

> *Three months:*

_____

_____

_____

> *Six months:*

_____

_____

_____

> *One year:*

_____

_____

_____

Write a letter to yourself with a vision of where you see yourself in three years and five years, starting with:

> It is _____ (a date three years from now) and I am experiencing my best life ever because… (List all the things you need to do in order to accomplish all of those goals.)

Consider putting away 25% of every commission check as if you are giving yourself a referral fee. This goes into a separate account to fund and invest in your business. You should have a separate bank account for business and a business credit card.

I also have an LLC (limited liability company) status for my business to keep it separate from my personal finances. You may want to discuss the advantages and disadvantages of an LLC with your accountant to determine if it would be beneficial for you.

5. PLAN TO BE PROFITABLE

If your goal is to be 40% profitable, you need to know, and track, your numbers. It's not what you make that counts; it's what you get to keep, and what you do with it.

So many of my counterparts earn huge sums of money; however, they are not profitable. They focus more on their egos than their profitability. It may be tempting to spend $10,000 on a big billboard with your name and picture on it, but is the return worth the investment? Make sure your marketing decisions are based on ROI, and not on seeing your name in lights.

While you're building your brand, allot 15% of your budget for marketing. As you become more established, and more successful, you can lower that to 10%.

Track everything, especially your ROI. If this is not your strength, hire someone who can do it for you. I now have a bookkeeper, and an accountant, in addition to my assistant, who writes my checks and keeps track of my expenses.

6. PAY OFF DEBTS; EMBRACE ABUNDANCE

While you are investing, you should also be paying off debt—preferably from the profits you make from your investments. Now this is where it gets tricky. I have learned that what you focus on tends to expand.

I don't want you to focus on your debt, because if that is what the "universe" hears you could just wind up with more debt. Your car breaks down, or the furnace goes out, and the money you saved needs to go towards those things.

Sure, shit happens. And it's good to be prepared in case of an emergency. However, bad things seem to happen to some people all of the time. That's because they are always focusing on the negative aspects of their lives: "Nothing ever goes well for me," or "If it's not one thing it's another," and so on.

Focus on abundance, and take the word "debt" out of your vocabulary. Practice positive affirmations: "Money flows to me like a steady stream," or "I am so grateful to live a life of abundance." This may sound "woo, woo". Just try it, and see how it works.

When you focus on abundance, the universe will provide everything you need and want. This is a belief system that works for those who can embrace it. The sky is the limit.

7. ADDRESS FINANCIAL INSECURITY

While I do believe in the power of having an abundant mentality, I have also suffered from financial insecurity my whole life (until recently).

I don't have a scarcity mentality. In fact, I am a very positive person. I simply never thought I had enough money. After reading about financial freedom in books by John Maxwell and Tony Robbins, I knew I could work toward, and achieve, "the numbers" I needed for financial security and independence. Aiming for something tangible made me feel better. I wouldn't be destitute in my old age after all.

It took doing a workshop with my friend and mentor, Maya Sela, for me to completely buy in to that concept emotionally. Maya lives and works in Israel. She invited me to participate in one of her workshops while I was there for a wedding.

This was something I had always wanted to do. I immediately signed up, not knowing what the workshop was about. I'm so glad I trusted my intuition. The subject was "Money is Energy." I spent the day with eight other women reflecting inwardly about my feelings toward money, from my childhood until today. I felt enlightened and empowered.

I came back home on July 9th, and on July 18th I did a Facebook live event for one of my listings. I have always admired this particular house, which I had sold to the sellers, who had lived there for five years. They had made tremendous improvements, and enhanced the house beautifully.

That night, my husband and I went to dinner with our dear friends, Ruth and Shimon, who live down the street from this particular house. We had just been with them at their daughter's wedding in Israel two weeks before. Shimon started talking about "the house on Coventry," and how he had always loved it.

He went on and on about the first floor master bedroom suite, the beautiful property, and the in-ground pool. I completely agreed with him and kept saying: "I know, I know, I love it too…" He turned to me and said, "So why don't you buy it?"

Aharon and I had just redone our kitchen, bathroom and dining room 18 months before, in the house we had lived in for 30 years. I glanced at Aharon, then looked back at Shimon and said, "Let's go take a look at it after dinner."

When we toured the house together, I was so excited I had butterflies in my stomach. I knew I was falling in love with it, even though I knew Aharon had never wanted to move. I turned to him and asked, "What do you think?"

This was an expensive house, with high taxes and heavy maintenance. I was sure he would say "No." To my surprise, he said "Let's do it." I was shocked. Back home, my fear of financial insecurity took over. Aharon went over finances with me and assured me we could swing it.

My recent workshop experience gave me the confidence I needed to go ahead and buy it. Ironically, even though it was my listing, another similar offer came in and thrust us into a crazy bidding war. Now, I had to have it; not because I had to win, but because I knew how sad I would be if I didn't live there now. It meant that much to me.

We moved into our new palatial home on December 1, 2018. It has changed my life, and the way I think and feel about money. I am no longer financially insecure, and I feel like I deserve the life Aharon and I have created together.

Chapter 9
Mentors, Coaches, and Building Teams

It takes honest self-awareness to build the team you need to achieve your financial, and overall career, goals.

It all starts with you: where you've come from, where you're heading, and how you plan to get there. Once you have a handle on your own progression, you will feel more confident building the right team to get you where you want to go.

We are all works in progress. The exercises in previous chapters have helped you build a strong foundation, with a better awareness of your core values and clear goals related to your 5 Pillars. You are now ready to catapult your business to the next level.

Who can you count on to help you get there? Who are your mentors? Who have you admired, and tried to emulate and learn from? I always try to surround myself with positive thinking people. Part of this is intuition, and part of it is luck.

I was blessed to begin my life with my mother as was my first mentor. Yaffa is a very wise and nurturing soul. Along the way, I have adopted many more mentors, who have helped me evolve into the person I strive to be.

It is very important to surround yourself with other successful people, and to seek opportunities to be mentored and to mentor others. In addition, find a coach who gets you, and knows how to guide you, and hold you accountable.

A coach is different than a mentor. When you pay someone to coach you it is a commitment to yourself to work toward reaching your goals one step at a time.

Sometimes you just need a different set of eyes and a new perspective into your life and your business. It's important to have someone ask pointed questions and not be afraid to call you on your bullshit—that is, all the things that hold you back or steer you in different directions. It's important to gain clarity so you can move forward.

There were no real estate coaches when I first started, so I followed other top agents and made them my mentors. I listened to the top agent in my office when she was talking on the phone. I watched how she dressed, how she behaved, and what she did to build her business.

I emulated a lot of what she did, just as many agents follow my lead today. She may not have volunteered to be my mentor, and it may have been tough for her to see me move up in rankings by using her approach. However, I will always be grateful for the bar she set for me.

Now that I find myself in a leadership position, I truly wish rising agents well and proactively mentor them. I realize mentoring someone else doesn't take away from my own success. It motivates me to step up my game when I see a colleague doing something well.

ACCESSING STAR POWER

I figured out early on that if I was going to commit to this business and pay a babysitter to watch my girls, I had to make my time in the office count. I needed to have a plan, and work with purpose to achieve my goals.

When a realtor in my office introduced me to the Star Power organization, and its founder, Howard Brinton, in 1993, it was a game changer. It truly changed my life.

I can truly say I attribute my quality of life, my course in life, and my ultimate success to Star Power, and all the people I've encountered there along the way. I have met some of my dearest friends at Star Power events. They have generously shared life lessons about what it takes to be successful in real estate, how to define success and, quite frankly, how to be a better person.

The Star Power format was brilliant and accessible. Every month, Howard Brinton, a dynamic realtor and educator, interviewed other successful realtors around the country. He had a talent for extracting the essence of what made these agents tick, so he could share exactly what they were doing to make their business successful. To me, he was the Barbara Walters of real estate interviewers.

For a monthly subscription fee, you would receive these interviews via cassette tape, along with a newsletter highlighting some of the most impactful points. I couldn't wait to get my tape every month. I popped them into the cassette player in my car, and listened to them over and over again. I learned about branding, marketing, prospecting, scripts, check lists, P&L statements, and how to grow a team with systems, from these top realtors, who are now my dear friends. You can still access the Star Power System online to learn from leading realtors, coaches and educators today.

After listening to these tapes for a few years, I decided to go to my first Star Power Conference in 1995, which was being held at the Ritz Carlton in Naples, Florida. My three daughters were all under nine years old. Aharon and my parents took care of the kids while I took off for a few days in Naples.

I couldn't afford the Ritz Carleton, so I stayed at another hotel about a mile down the road. I didn't know many people there, which motivated me to meet and socialize with other conference attendees.

I was excited to see that all the "stars" from the interviews I had been listening to were there. They not only attended the conference on their own dime, they spoke at classes with no payment. They were happy to share whatever they could, and they were there to learn from each other.

It was the most wonderful sharing community I had ever encountered. Back in the office, and in my local real estate community, no one was willing to talk about what they were doing to succeed. Realtors can be insecure. They worry about their colleagues stealing their ideas and their clients. They hesitate to share ideas that may take business away from them.

The Star Power realtors were different. They were generous speakers, and teachers, who freely shared whatever you wanted to know, one-on-one, before or after class. Even conversations in the ladies room could turn into inspirational idea sessions.

Everyone came from different real estate companies, and nobody cared what color flag you were with. They shared ideas, costs, vendor names, check lists, and whatever else they were doing freely, and most importantly, happily.

SEIZING OPPORTUNITY

I discovered there was another agent from my area staying at the Ritz Carlton. Her name was Gheeta Khana. She invited me to hang out with her, and introduced me to some of the "stars" she knew. I felt so lucky to be included.

One of the stars invited Gheeta to crash a black tie dinner dance, which was a paid event, and just show up for the dancing. She invited me to come along. I had not anticipated this, and didn't pack anything appropriate for a black tie affair. She encouraged me to go anyway, and told me to find something to wear.

My mother taught me you don't have to spend a lot of money to have a sense of style and look like a million bucks. I looked at what I had brought with me and put together a killer outfit.

I wore a black one piece bathing suit with black mesh on top, a pair of black spandex shorts, and a new black t-shirt from a flea market that I bought for $10. The t-shirt had been cut up with geometric designs. I thought I might use it as a cover up over my bathing suit. Little did I know it would complete my outfit. I put the peekaboo t-shirt over the bathing suit and shorts like a mini dress, and wore a pair of stiletto high-heeled shoes.

Everyone asked me where I had bought my outfit—even the Ritz Carlton waitresses working the function commented on it. I laughed to myself, and called my mother later to tell her what a hit my flea market outfit was. You have to own it, baby, and walk like you own the place.

I'm so grateful that I seized this opportunity as an entrée into a world that I wanted, and needed, to be a part of. Gheeta was there for me, to make this crucial connection, which I will always be grateful for.

It's important to step outside of your comfort zone. This was a crucial step for me. It helped catapult me to where I am today.

Choosing the Right People for the Right Jobs

I attended all the classes, breakout sessions and general sessions at the conference, and wrote pages and pages of notes. When I returned home, I immediately started implementing what I had learned. This is key!

You must implement what you learn at conferences and seminars, otherwise it's a waste of time and money. I had listened to the tapes since 1992, and had already hired my first assistant only five years after getting into real estate. This conference taught me how to get to the next level, and how much more I could do with a licensed assistant.

My assistant, Cathy, who has been with me since 1993, didn't want to get her real estate license because she had four children at home, and didn't want the responsibility. So I had to hire another assistant. I put a want ad in my monthly newsletter that goes out to the entire town saying:

> Only you know if you want to work with "Only Orly" – licensed or willing to get licensed.

"Only Orly" is a tagline I started using around 1989, after I learned about the benefits of taglines at a Hobbs/Herder marketing class. No one in my area was doing this at the time, and a lot of people smirked and talked about me behind my back when I started marketing myself as "Only" Orly.

In the long run, I'm glad I listened to my mother, who told me to drop Steinberg and be "Only Orly". She was right. I'm glad I listened to her and followed my heart, instead of being swayed by others.

Two candidates, who needed to be licensed, applied from my community. Since I didn't have the hiring skills or experience to know which one would be a better fit, I decided to hire them both temporarily and see how things progressed.

Earlier in my career, I had read "The Platinum Rule" by Tony Alessandra and Michael J. O'Conner, which explains four distinct personality types and how to determine their dominant characteristics. I make sure all of my team members also read, and understand, this book.

THE FOUR PERSONALITY TYPES: D-I-S-C

First, you need to become familiar with how different personality types think, work and interact with others. What motivates them? What do they find rewarding? What could they add to your team? How should you approach them as a client? This can be a real game changer when you are building teams. I now ask all potential hires to take a DISC personality assessment:

1. "D" represents dominance: These "Directors" are firm, forceful, confident, competitive, decisive, and determined risk-takers. They can be impatient, and speak loudly and quickly.

2. "I" represents influence: These "Socializers," are outgoing, optimistic, enthusiastic people, who like to be at the center of things. They love to talk, especially about themselves, and are the life of the party.

3. "S" represents steadiness: These "Relators" are nurturing, team players, who like stability and care greatly about relationships with others. They are likable, but sometimes timid and slow to change. They love to help people.

4. "C" represents conscientiousness: These "Thinkers" are self-controlled and cautious. They are very analytical, and slow to make decisions and pull the trigger. They are very detail oriented and make great accountants.

The key take-away for me is that while the golden rule we were all raised with says we should treat others the way we would like to be treated, the "platinum rule" says: treat people the way "they" want to be treated. Since we are in a people business, it's important—if not crucial—to know how to treat people the way they want to be treated.

One of my new assistants, Megan, had an "S" personality. She was very quiet, timid, and unsure of herself. Conversely, Noreen had an "I-D" personality, and took the initiative to ask questions about how to do things. She was also friends with my longtime assistant, Cathy.

Noreen had a "can do" attitude, and was eager to learn. Working with her taught me to always hire for attitude first. Skills can be taught; attitude cannot. And by the way, you really can't fix stupid.

I have hired people who just didn't get it and never will. You can't make people what they are not. Over time, I have learned to hire slowly and fire quickly. If someone has the right attitude, and basic skills, you can teach them the rest. If they don't, it's best to cut ties and move on amicably.

Cathy and Noreen served on the local PTO (parent teacher organization) together. I have found that people who are active in PTOs are great candidates for administrative positions. They are generally team players, who are dedicated to nurturing and serving others. They tend to have flexible schedules and stable home lives. They enjoy working with people, and are good at multi-tasking. They are usually well connected in the community, and can bring you leads. Both Cathy and Noreen fit those profiles.

Noreen became my first buyer's agent/admin. I do not recommend combining these positions. I have tried it twice and it failed both times. They are different jobs, and should be treated that way. An admin is a salaried position, while a buyer's agent works on commission. These roles also require different skill sets.

Originally, when I combined those positions, I wasn't sure I had enough work to hire another admin, and I was still working with both buyers and sellers. I didn't think I'd have enough additional buyer's leads to keep Noreen busy. Plus, I was already paying Cathy for about 25 hours a week. I thought I could save money, and keep Noreen fully occupied with this role. But pulling people in too many directions doesn't work.

Noreen was phenomenal both as a buyer's agent and as an admin. She sold her first house at the first Open House she ever did, to a man named Bob Philhower. He came to town for a cup of coffee at Dunkin Donuts, wandered into her Open House, and bought it.

Unfortunately, over time, Noreen started getting burned out working seven days a week. After a few years, she told me it was too much for her and she wanted to be my full time client care coordinator, with a focus on marketing.

I was nervous about this. It would mean adding a fulltime salaried position. I agreed, with the provision that Noreen would help me find a buyer's agent to take over her role. She recommended a client, Carol Conger, who had just been laid off from her job. Carol got her real estate license, and has been working with my team for more than 18 years now. She is an amazing buyer's agent.

The lesson there is: a great team member will push you to the next level and help you grow.

NEXT LEVEL TEAM BUILDING

After Noreen settled into her new marketing role, she proved to be a valuable asset at the Star Power conferences. We had fun learning together, and meeting other realtors with similar challenges. We both got excited about similar things, we collaborated, and we implemented ideas as partners with complete buy-in.

Noreen could see where I was going with my business. We became an effective team, pulling in the same direction.

It is extremely important to get all of your team members to buy in to everything you do after going to a conference. One year, four of us participated in a Star Power conference in Washington, DC. I was so excited about taking my already successful business to the next level that my mind was going a million miles a minute with all the new ideas in my head. I could barely sleep.

I woke up at 3 am after the second day of sessions, and went to the bathroom so I wouldn't disturb Noreen, who was sharing my room. I wrote pages and pages of notes about everything I wanted to implement. I went back to sleep, and when I woke up for the day I told Noreen about how early I'd been up taking notes.

She laughed and said she had done the same thing. She was up at 4 am, and had a bunch of notes as well. We were so excited, and couldn't wait to get back home and implement our new ideas. You can't pay someone enough to have that kind of dedication and excitement. Noreen has always had my back and my best interests at heart. I am truly blessed to have her on my team.

I was so glad that two of our buyer's agents, Carol Conger and Mary Rambone, also participated in that conference. They, too, were excited about what they had learned and were motivated to put new concepts to work to grow our business. I knew I had complete buy-in from my team, and that they were ready to grow to the next level together.

The right team is everything. It is so important to choose new members wisely. I want to work with people who have my back, are clear about their role, and are committed to doing what it takes to make our business succeed. I want them to know that I'm invested in their success as well.

Each person needs to buy in to your vision and lift you up. You shouldn't have to pull people in the direction you want to go. The right people will push you to the next level.

When Noreen retired, I had enough confidence to know what works for our team. I put my trust in Tracey, who had automatic buy-in from day one. Tracey lives in town. She knew who I was, and respected and admired my work. It was an easy sell, on both sides. She took us all to an even higher level, infusing new systems and excitement into our already dedicated team.

Chapter 10
Building a Business Foundation; Putting Systems in Place

If you build your team right, and put strong systems in place, you shouldn't always have to be there to make sure everything runs smoothly. Building a strong business foundation took time and trust. Now, I can relax while I'm away, and I'm confident in our ability to shift and thrive in the midst of change.

For example, when my client care coordinator, Noreen, announced her retirement after being an integral part of our team for almost 22 years, it could have been devastating. I knew she would be difficult to replace.

I used to introduce Noreen to clients as my right hand and my left brain. We finished each other's sentences, and very often she gave clients the same exact advice using the same words. I told clients she was 95% my clone, and she would be in the office 40-50 hours a week answering their questions, managing transactions, and running my business when I was away.

Whenever I traveled, Noreen ran the business as if I was there. This gave me the freedom, and the luxury, to enjoy a relaxing reprieve, and not be stressed about the office. I could go away for three weeks or more, and know that everything would run smoothly.

In fact, I left Noreen to run my business, soup to nuts, while I was in Israel for three weeks, right after she joined the team in April, 1996.

This was before cell phones and internet connections, which now make it so easy to reach people around the world. She was, understandably, a bit concerned. However, I put her mind at ease with this philosophy: the worst thing that can happen is that a deal falls apart. And I'm OK with that. I still am.

It was more important for me to be with my family, creating memories and enjoying ourselves in Israel. I knew I would always cherish this time together; however, I probably wouldn't remember if a potential sale fell apart. Thankfully, we didn't lose any business while I was away. Noreen handled everything beautifully.

I believe in "baptism by fire." If you throw someone who you know is capable into a challenging situation, they will rise to the occasion. If you trust people, and let them know you believe in them, they will trust themselves and step up to the task at hand.

As our team grew, Noreen and I realized we needed more structure and systems to manage the business and provide consistent customer service to our clients. We went to many conferences and seminars together to learn as much as we could. We developed amazing systems that have allowed our business to grow and hum smoothly most of the time.

Looking for Noreen's replacement was not an easy, or enjoyable, task. As soon as she made her official announcement, we immediately placed an ad on Indeed.com and started scrubbing the myriad of resumes that came in.

Finding the Right Replacement

We use the DISC personality profile test for everyone we hire, which identifies four prevailing traits:

- Dominance – direct, strong-willed, and forceful
- Influence – sociable, talkative, and lively
- Steadiness – gentle, accommodating, and soft-hearted
- Conscientiousness – private, analytical, and logical

I'm a "DI" personality. Noreen is an "ID". I wanted an "I-S-C" personality for this position: "I" for people skills, "S" for the nurturing required to deal with anxious clients, and "C" to handle all the details and paperwork.

Neither Noreen nor I have much "C" in us, although Noreen did her best to keep up with the paperwork, and she did it well. She thought this combination would be hard to find. I knew it existed, and that this was what I needed to take the team to the next level.

I received tons of resumes. Only one of them looked promising. This person had a lot of administrative experience in real estate, yet was not licensed. Noreen's phone interview with Tracey went very well. The next step was the DISC personality test. Low and behold, she came up "I–S –C."

Tracey lives in my town, and knew me by reputation. I thought this was too good to be true; however, I believed I had once again manifested exactly what I was looking for.

It took Noreen less than a week to train Tracey, using our policy and procedure manual. The manual has a checklist for everything we do: getting ready for Monday Morning Madness and our team meeting;

what to do for a new listing; putting a property under contract; getting a house ready for closing; and more.

After hosting a wonderful retirement luncheon for Noreen on December 28, Tracey started her new position on January 2, 2019. She was very excited to get started and dove right in.

On Monday, January 7, I held a mini advance for my team to kick off the New Year. Some people call these retreats, but I prefer to look forward. We went over our team goals and I gave them the latest book I was reading: "The One Word," by Dan Britton. I knew it was going to be a busy week. I had more than 10 listings hitting the market, and Jill, my marketing manager, was out with the flu.

So with a new transaction coordinator, and no marketing manager, I called my outside vendor/professional photographer to at least start taking pictures of the new listings. Tracey suggested we recruit her daughter, Amanda, who had some experience putting listings into the MLS, and was home from college.

We launched three listings that week without a hitch, set up more pictures, and prepped five more listings so that when Jill came in she would hit the ground running. The following week, January 13–18, I went on a pre-planned vacation and left Tracey to run the office on the second week of her job.

Tracey not only survived a very challenging first two weeks with Jill and me not around, she successfully helped put seven new listings under contract with offers flooding in from other agents. Our checklists and manual provided her with a guide to follow. This was a true testament to the success of good systems.

Our team had already been more or less cross-trained, to ensure we wouldn't be left paralyzed when someone was out. After being short staffed during Tracey's first two weeks, I realized we needed even more cross-training. This gave me an opportunity to identify holes in our systems and address them. For example, I now provide more detailed descriptions of listings coming on the market to make it easier for my team to launch them effectively.

I call these crazy busy, short-staffed, situations working in triage mode. When you can only deal with issues that need your most immediate attention, you figure out what is most important. In this mode, you have to be comfortable enough with your team's abilities to be able to let go, revisit things later, and identify where improvements are needed. Use these opportunities to grow, and learn how to work smarter, so you're better prepared next time.

Chapter 11
Running Your Business like a Business; And it is a Business

Most agents—no matter how long they have been realtors—don't have a consistent, predictable, or sustainable business model. That's because most of us were never taught how to run a business. There is often no accountability, no discipline, and no real guidance within the real estate realm.

When I started working as a real estate agent, there were very few resources available to guide me. Most agents don't know enough about running a business to serve as mentors, and there is no definitive manual or "holy grail". While some colleagues may offer dribs and drabs of helpful advice, very few are open to sharing much of what they do.

There are more books available now than when I started. Back then, we had Tom Hopkins, Dale Carnegie, Zig Zigler, and Danielle Kennedy. Now there is also John C. Maxwell, Stephen Covey, Gary Keller, Tom Ferry, Michael Maher, and more. (See reading list). Many of these authors also offer great coaching programs. Explore your options. Find what resonates for you, and implement a model that will work in your market.

The most important thing is to do what you love to do. You will flourish from there. There are so many ways to get business. Real estate prospecting can be like a Chinese menu: you can take two from column

A and two from column B, so to speak. The key is to find five or more things you enjoy doing, do them consistently, and do them well.

GENERATE LEADS

People often ask me how I average six-eight appointments per week, and get 80% of my listings from "Come List Me" calls.

What do you need to do to get those six appointments per week? When did sellers start calling me directly? Here are some actions you can take to build your brand awareness:

Mailings – This is a lead generating system for sellers, and it's a numbers game. If you are just starting to mail to a geographic farm neighborhood, start with a minimum of 500 mailings every 21 days for the first six months. Then you can scale back to every 30 days. It is costly, and takes about six months to start reaping the benefits. It can be worth it if you stick with it. Believe it or not, direct mail still works in this new age world.

I usually do EDDM (Every Door Direct Mail) mailings for lower postage costs. You can find more information on the USPS website.

Grow your geographic farm – I started mailing to a geographic farm very early in my career and haven't stopped. I started with 200 homes, then 500, 1,000, 2,000, and eventually I began mailing to the entire town of 4,400 homes. Then I added a second, neighboring town of about 5,000 homes, which grew my leads exponentially. This allowed me to brand myself so effectively, that people started seeking me out.

Several years ago, when I wanted to expand my market further, I took on a new town of 4,200, and it took six months to generate my first call. A year later, I had seven percent of that town's market share. Patience is key. Like any kind of farming, it will take time for your crops to grow so that you can reap the benefits.

Your Database – Mine the gold in your own database. It should include the names of every contact you have ever done business with, everyone who has ever referred business to you, and everyone you know, basically.

Organize your data base according to your relationship with each person. Begin with the end in mind. Think about how you will want to pull up resources and reach out to a group of people, based on their contact type. For instance, one person can fall under several categories: all buyers; buyers in a specific town; and buyers who are on my VIP list. I have similar categories for sellers, referrals, vendors, colleagues, professional networking contacts, etc.

You should have a "VIP" system to connect with special past clients at least once a month. I have kept my listing intake sheets since the late 1990s, and I still call homeowners I've done a comparative market analysis (CMA) for regularly. Many of these potential sellers still haven't moved and appreciate my call; others say they will call me when they are ready to re-engage.

Create a calendar and schedule an action plan. Call, text, email, do a giveaway, host a client appreciation party, or invite them to an event or seminar. Be creative. Make it useful. Have fun with it.

Which database is the best? The one you will actually use consistently is the one that is best for you. I have used Top Producer since 1993; however, there are plenty of options. Do your research. Ask questions. Monitor results.

Expired and FSBO Leads – There is gold to be mined here, too. Make a plan. Set up a system for pulling up names every day. Get phone numbers. Write a series of letters. Practice scripts to convert expired and FSBO (for sale by owner) sellers who have already raised their hands to say they are ready to sell. Show them the benefits of working with you.

There are many programs that teach you how to convert FSBOs and expireds. They include systems and scripts you can master.

Work Expired Listings – Mailing campaigns to expired listings have worked well for me. They have already raised their hands to say they need, or want, to sell. They have already committed to paying a realtor's commission, unlike an FSBO. Now you just have to convince them to list with you.

This is where your listing skills come in: know your local market numbers; perfect your listing presentation; and practice effective scripts.

Online Referral Sources – There are many online referral sources available. Some are better than others.

Choose one that matches your needs, your business model, and your budget. For instance, if you are a single agent who uses BoomTown, and you can't handle the leads generated, you will lose time, energy and money.

Finding the right fit may take some trial and error. Don't be afraid to experiment. Here are a few options:

- BoomTown
- Qazzoo.com
- ReferralExchange
- HomeLight
- UpNest
- Zillow
- Realtor.com
- Homes.com

- VerifiedLeads.com
- FastExpert
- Agent Pronto
- Veterans United Realty

I'm sure there are many others. Referral services are always soliciting agents. Make sure to do your homework before signing any long term contracts. And don't pay anything until you have closed. At that time, the referral fee is usually 25%.

Some of the other popular online lead resources may also be a good investment if you are one of the top three-five realtors in your zip code.

These sites produce better results in some areas than others, so give it six months before you evaluate whether or not it is working for you. Make sure you are equipped to jump on leads in the first three minutes, or train people on your team to respond right away to convert leads to appointments.

Open Houses – Open houses are still a viable form of lead generation, whether they are in person or virtual, a format perfected during the COVID-19 virus quarantine.

Keep in mind, these showcases are better for finding potential buyers early on in the process, since most committed buyers will have already found an agent to guide them.

If you are going to invest your time and energy into hosting an open house, make it as effective as possible. Start by extending a special invitation to neighbors. You can call them, or put cards in their mailboxes inviting them to a neighborhood preview an hour before the general public. Step it up by serving refreshments and providing handouts, which could lead to additional neighborhood listings.

Host a Facebook live event or post a video inviting everyone to attend. Put up good signage everywhere you can think of—the more the better—and be sure to remove it as soon as the open house is over.

Establish a makeshift office at a table, with brochures about the house and your business. Ask attendees to sign in on an iPad so you have accurate, legible information, including email addresses for your data base. Consider having a mortgage professional there for immediate pre-approvals.

You can host a more elaborate open house for a high end, luxury home. Make it a twilight party. Hire a musician and have it catered. Invite other realtors. Make it open to the public, or cultivate a more exclusive guest list. Be creative. Show sellers you are willing to do more to truly showcase their homes.

Be casual and friendly when you introduce yourself. Engage people in conversation to make them feel comfortable. Establish rapport by asking casual questions while you tour the house together. Avoid hard sell tactics. There is an art to converting someone to work with you. Own it. Make it yours.

Always follow up immediately with a note or email. Leave a nice note for the seller, too, thanking them for allowing you to host their open house. Let them know what kind of activity you had.

Social Media – What are you doing on social media to promote yourself and your business? Are you placing targeted ads, posting Facebook videos, doing Facebook live sessions, or creating a presence on LinkedIn, Instagram, etc.?

Put a consistent plan in place: know what you are going to do, when, and how often. There are companies that can do this for you; however, sometimes their work looks too generic. The public needs to see, and get to know, the real you.

Community Events – Be active in your community. Network and join organizations that speak to your heart: chamber of commerce, planning board, PTO, etc.

Give back with charitable fundraisers. About 15 years ago, I started an annual shredding event where I donate a 10 ton shredding truck that is accessible to the entire community. I do a mass mailing, which brings in more than 400 people, who also bring non-perishable food for the local food bank. This is paying it forward at its best.

Knock on Doors – This is not something I like to do; however, this old school method still works for some agents.

Cold/Warm Calling – A cold call involves reaching out to someone you've never spoken to before. These phone numbers could come from purchased lists.

A warm call could be anyone you have a connection with, starting with people in your data base. You could reach out to everyone you've ever done a market analysis for. You could revisit all buyer leads you've ever received. You could also contact business associates you met through networking organizations.

Real estate is a numbers game. The more people you call, the more leads you'll get. The more appointments you schedule, the more contracts you can close.

Network and Earn Referrals – I also receive "Come List Me" calls through realtor referrals, personal referrals, and past clients. I make a point of referring my clients to the best realtors around the country, and have built up a wonderful network of top agents. I believe it is important to serve as my client's resource for all of their real estate needs.

My VIP program enables me to stay in touch with past clients on a monthly basis using a series of emails, note cards, client events, mailings, and calls at least twice a year. I also incorporate my adoptees—buyers who bought my listings through another realtor—into the VIP program so I can stay in touch with them as well. Often, I get calls from my adoptees years later. In their minds, I have been their agent all along.

As you can see, there are many ways to generate leads. Pick a few that you like, do them well, and do them consistently. If one thing doesn't work, try something else. You don't need to do them all.

DECIDE WHEN TO BUILD A TEAM

People often ask: "When is a good time to start building a team?" I would say that after you make about 25 – 30 transactions a year, you should consider getting some administrative help to take all the paperwork and day-to-day minutia off of your plate.

You are the talent. You should be spending most of your time with clients, converting leads, closing deals, and negotiating. That is your sweet spot. Once you have someone reliable in place to handle the crucial "busy work," your business should grow at least 25%. Then, it will be time to add a buyer's agent to show and sell more homes.

Each hire should increase your business by 25% or more. For every 50 – 70 transactions per year, you can add another administrative person and another buyer's agent. This is my formula. It is not cut in stone; however, you want to make sure you don't lose customer service as you do more and more transactions.

My mantra has always been: Learn, implement, grow, sustain. Learn, implement, grow, sustain. Learn, implement, grow, sustain.

First, learn how to grow your business. Implement as much as you can. As you grow your business, make sure what you are implementing is sustainable. Rinse, repeat, and repeat again, as you grow your business to the next level.

Chapter 12
Conquering FOMO; Keeping it Real

Once your business is at the next level, and just when you think you've arrived, FOMO hits you. What are you missing?

Many of us, if not all of us, suffer from the syndrome called FOMO— Fear of Missing Out.

Social media makes it so easy to get caught up in other people's lives. We are all comparing ourselves to one another every day. Who is doing what? Who is going where? We follow people achieving all kinds of things. It all looks great on the surface. And hopefully it is great for them. But only you know what is best for you and your lifestyle.

FOMO is also prevalent at high powered real estate conferences and other meetings featuring high achievers who stand out for one reason or another. After going to many of them, I can certainly attest to the value of these worthwhile, educational events. It's wonderful to learn, grow, get inspired and be motivated by speakers and panels of top agents and other attendees. However, it is also very easy to get swept away in other people's agendas.

You might be selling 20, 50 or 100 homes a year and get deflated when you hear about people doing 300, 500 or 800 transactions a year. You might feel like you're not enough, you're not doing enough, and you're not worthy to even be here.

Did you ever think about what it takes to do all those transactions? Think about the hours you need to devote to doing the business, leading the team and having enough manpower to manage that many units. And what about the expenses?

It is not what you make that counts, it is what you get to keep at the end of the day. There is a cost, and a price to pay, for everything you do in life. You need to know yourself and be clear about what you want, and how far you want to go. Some will reach for the stars, while others will be equally satisfied with much less.

CONFERENCE PREP

Before I leave for a conference, I always assess my business, and my life, by asking the following questions:

- **Where am I right now in my life?**
- **Where do I want to be, both personally and professionally?**
- **Am I at goal?**
- **What are my goals?**
  - More time for family?
  - More business? How much more?
  - More travel?
  - More investments?
  - More hobbies?
  - More money? If so, what for, specifically?
- **How do I want to achieve these goals?**
  - Expand my team?
  - Implement better systems?
  - Use technology?
  - Do more marketing? What kind?

This helps me figure out what I am listening for in this particular conference, and enables me to get the information, and motivation, I need to accomplish specific goals.

FOLLOW YOUR AGENDA; IMPLEMENT WHAT WORKS FOR YOU

Going into a conference with a clear agenda helps filter out the "white noise" so you can choose sessions wisely, save your energy for the topics that will help you achieve your goals, and have fun meeting new people and absorbing new ideas without putting pressure on yourself to do too much. My tips below come from years of experience. I hope they will help you skip a few steps along the way.

LISTEN SELECTIVELY:

Conferences are packed with information. Listen and take notes that are relevant to your business today. Focus on ideas that will get you to your own next level. Too many ideas and "to do's" can be overwhelming; you'll probably go back to your business and not implement any of them. Listen to those top realtors who honestly share what works and what doesn't.

DEBRIEF:

Stay an extra day to relax, debrief, and get your plan of action in place. Take some time to have some fun. Connect with friends who you can debrief and brainstorm with. Don't hurry back to your reality. This time out is super important to re-focus on your life and your business.

STAY TRUE TO YOU:

It's easy to get carried away by someone else's agenda. You can feel the energy in the room, and before you know it you are getting pumped up by yet another marketing initiative. Or you may just start thinking your goals should align with another attendee's, because they just sound so good.

Orly Steinberg "Only Orly"

Take a deep breath and put those healthy blinders on to stay focused and filter what you are listening to. When you stay focused on your own agenda, you can listen more actively and identify things that speak to your own goals.

Without a doubt, the energy at conferences can be contagious. Take a moment to consider what is driving you. Why are you there? Is it ego? Or is it your true desire to fulfill your goals?

The agent on stage who is doing 1,000 transactions a year could be single, in debt, and have a need to feed a huge ego. I'm not saying this is always the case, as I have many realtor friends who are killing it in business while maintaining wonderful lives and relationships. Just be aware: if you don't know a speaker's back story, you should be wary about taking what they say at face value. Take away what will work for you and your lifestyle.

RE-EVALUATE YOUR "HAVE TO"; RE-INVENT YOUR WHY

Some people have more ego, more drive, and more of an "I have to" than others. One is not necessarily better than another. It's important to be honest with yourself, and evaluate what is right for you.

Several years ago, I spoke to a select group of top-producing residential real estate agents from across North America at a REV (Real Estate Vision) conference. My topic was "How Much Is Enough?"

I noticed that many of my peers who have been in the business 30 years or so, and are still doing very well, were still striving to do even more. Since I fit into this category, I felt the need to know how much was enough for me. I figured others would like to explore this, too.

My presentation was guided by the questions Tony Robbins asks in his book, "Money Matters." Robbins emphasizes how important it is to know how to achieve financial freedom. First, you need to know what your "number" is. I asked the group if they knew theirs. Then, we discussed how to determine the amount of passive income we need to give us the financial freedom we want. It's different for everyone.

I have often asked myself why I was getting caught up in somebody else's goals and dreams. Why did I feel I was lacking? Why didn't I think I was enough? What is enough for me? Finding the answers to those questions, in a shifting landscape, has become a life journey.

Several years ago, I felt like I had lost my "I have to." I had already achieved most of my financial and personal goals; however, I didn't feel fulfilled. I had lost my drive and passion as well.

When I first started working in real estate, and the girls were very young, we needed a larger home to expand our family of four. That was my first, and biggest, "I have to." Then I had to pay down our mortgage and debt, save money to pay for three college tuitions and weddings, and purchase real estate investments to produce passive retirement income.

All of a sudden, in 2015 I found myself debt free, with no more college tuition to pay, and enough passive income to live comfortably. This was a good place to be; however, I started feeling depressed because I lost my drive and sense of purpose. I started journaling more than ever to gain clarity about what was really important to me and reading motivational, reflective books by John Maxwell, Hal Elrod, and many others listed in the back of this book.

CHECKING IN

While I was re-evaluating my purpose, and striving for a mindset reset, I asked myself so many questions. How would you answer these questions for yourself?

- **Where am I right now in my life?**

_____

_____

_____

- **What gives me joy?**

_____

_____

_____

- **How are my relationships? Truly?**

_____

_____

_____

- **What is missing?**

_____

_____

_____

I reflected on my relationship with Aharon. I wondered: "Are we truly connecting, or are we going out to dinner because I don't feel like cooking tonight, and we're calling it a date night?"

I considered my relationships with my daughters. They're adults now. How well do I know them? Are we deeply connecting? Do we spend enough quality time together?

My parents are now in their late 80s, and their health is starting to fail. I know I want to appreciate and enjoy more time with them. How can I make a more conscious effort to do that?

CONTROL YOUR CALENDAR; BEFORE IT CONTROLS YOU

I realized during this time of reflection, that I had been given the gift of time, and the financial freedom to determine how I spend it.

You can either fill up your calendar with things you love to do, or your calendar will fill up with things you feel obligated to do, but don't want to. It's up to you to figure out how to balance the things you love to do and the things you know you must do.

Now I ask myself: What have I always wanted to do, yet have never felt I had the time to do?

This is my time to do what truly brings me joy: yoga, art, reading more, writing this book, coaching, traveling, and taking classes. It took me a few years to figure this out and, most of all, give myself permission to earn less money and put more joy back into my life. In the process, I actually started earning more money because I was on the right path for me.

This is a very difficult thing for a competitive overachiever to do. I can be an all, or nothing, kind of person. I even thought about retirement. And then what?

I thought deeply about my next steps, and realized I could incorporate all of my interests and passions into my existing career and be OK with what came next. My new outlook gave me new passion and drive to expand my team with more buyer's agents who can show and sell to buyers while I focus on the sellers.

I sold my last buyers a house in early 2017, and I haven't looked back. I'm enjoying having more control of my time as I focus exclusively on seller appointments. I can spend weekends with my family, and I am taking the time to do all of the things that truly bring me joy.

I am still a work in progress, as we all are until the day we die, and I am enjoying the ride immensely. What can you adjust to enjoy your life more?

Chapter 13
Facing Real Estate Challenges; Mindset Matters

We all wake up some mornings asking ourselves: Why am I in this business? Why do I put myself through all of these ups and downs?

Our income is uncertain, and working with some clients can be very challenging. And yet, there are some very tangible rewards. Ultimately, like everything else, it comes down to mindset. What are you choosing to focus on?

Imagine this visual: Whenever I'm on a plane, before I connect to the WiFi or start working on my laptop, I like to take a moment to assess my life from a bird's eye view. Looking down at the clouds stretching out below me gives me an opportunity to reflect on different areas of my life with a new perspective.

You can recreate this exercise anywhere, at any time. Start by focusing on the big picture. How do you see your life, your legacy, your reputation, and your relationships? How do they unfold, intersect, or stand alone?

Keeping all of this in mind makes it easier to overcome challenges as they arise. Ask yourself: In the scheme of things, how will this affect me? Am I doing the right thing? Am I being true to my core values?

OVERCOMING CHALLENGES 101: LISTEN

Real estate is about service, consultation, and approaching people with respect, compassion, and a willingness to listen. Good communication skills are the key to good relationships. In the end, it won't be your great salesmanship that will win over your clients. It will be your ability to listen to them.

Hidden, underlying agendas can drive people towards, or away from, buying or selling a house despite what they initially tell you. Truly listen to what your clients are saying, and sometimes, what they are not saying. Listen with the intention of understanding their needs, fears and challenges. Listen to their heart and soul.

Always return all calls, even if you don't have an answer. Sometimes people just want to be heard. They want someone to understand what they're saying, or what they're going through. Everyone deserves your attention, and the courtesy of a call back. That may sound simple, but it's not always easy.

TELL THE TRUTH; MANAGE YOUR TIME

Be authentic. Sometimes you need to tell a seller what they need to hear, not what they want to hear. Make sure to highlight the positives and deal with the negatives head on. Don't try to sweep issues under the rug. Nine times out of ten, I will get a listing because the seller knows I'm speaking the truth, and not just trying to get their business. They see that I am looking at the big picture, with their best interests at heart, and not just focusing on a sale.

Honor people's time. Always be on time as a sign of respect. What is your mindset on time? Are you perpetually late? Does time get away from you while you are busy working on something or trying to fit in one more thing?

Some people are always early. Some people are always late. It's a choice. Think about how it affects others.

DEALS WILL GO SOUTH; BE PREPARED

Real estate transactions fall apart for a myriad of reasons. Most of them are not your fault. You can, however, control how you respond to situations that don't proceed as planned.

Think about all of the things that could affect a listing or sale:

- Inspection issues
- Appraisal issues
- Mortgage issues
- Buyer's Remorse
- Couples fight and break up
- Parents see a house and convince a young couple not to buy it
- Clients get stuck standing on principle instead of looking at the big picture
- Negotiation of chattel and fixtures such as refrigerators, pool tables, etc.

There will be days when it seems every deal is going south, or has challenges. Clients just want to vent and blame you for everything. People turn on you because things aren't going their way, and you happen to be a convenient punching bag.

We all have stories. I could share many. For example, when a bitter spouse's frustration in the middle of a divorce spills over to you, it can get nasty. It's not pleasant. I've been there.

When someone knows they are losing their house because of financial issues, they may feel you are the only thing standing between their beloved home and what they know they must do to get out of their financial situation. It's not easy to sell a house you love, and can no longer afford. It's easy to take things out on the realtor.

This is where your mindset, and your ability to distance yourself from a situation, comes in. I have a few tried and true techniques for dealing with those days.

First, I use the "five minute rule." I voice my frustrations and disappointments for five minutes out loud, and then force myself to move on and let it go. This is a practice. It doesn't come easily; however, with enough practice it can be mastered.

Second, I try to see how I can learn and grow from a situation, both personally and professionally. I think of potential solutions and see if there are systems I can put into place to avoid similar situations in the future. Who do I want to be when I am in this kind of situation? How can I serve those around me better?

When you're prepared, you can handle just about anything. For instance, now when a client calls and wants to know if the buyer's deposit money or a mortgage commitment is in, I can respond calmly instead of scrambling for an answer, because my team has documented all of that information both in an excel spread sheet and in Top Producer.

At the end of the day, it's all about attitude and gratitude—knowing you have everything you want and need so you can do the best you can for your clients, regardless of the outcome. When I am really frustrated, and a difficult client is venting at me relentlessly, I remind myself that I have a beautiful, relaxing home and a loving husband to go home to. If all else fails, I may leave the office for some retail therapy, go see my grandchildren, or just do something fun.

My mantra, which I have taught my team is: "I have a home." This helps us detach from a client's drama and not become so emotionally involved in each transaction. Of course we care; however, we need to move on with our lives and appreciate what we have in order to help others.

KNOW WHEN TO LET GO

Working with really difficult clients is always a challenge. First, try to determine if they are difficult because of their needs, because they don't understand the process, or because they are just a jerk. We have all worked with jerks, and sometimes they are just not worth it. Sometimes we just need to push the delete button and say "Next!"

A truly difficult person who just isn't getting it can drag you down like an albatross around your neck, whether they are a buyer or a seller. As a new agent, you may want to continue working with a difficult person because you think they may eventually buy or sell. With experience, you gain the confidence to let people go so you can free up energy for 10 new clients who will be a pleasure to work with.

I had one particularly difficult seller, who had some toes amputated from diabetes and was just a miserable person. Even his family had a hard time dealing with him. After his house had been on the market for several weeks, he started getting frustrated. Nothing I could do was going to be good enough. He didn't want to acknowledge the negative feedback he was getting from potential buyers, and he started blaming me for everything. I realized I was just a convenient punching bag.

I swore that when this transaction closed I would buy a gold diamond bracelet I had seen at my friend's jewelry store to compensate myself. He was so nasty that I looked at a matching necklace, too.

When we finally got an offer, he bragged about how he had negotiated deals in the millions when he was working. I told him the only difference between him and me were a few "0s."

If the house hadn't closed when it did, I was going to ask my friend for a matching ankle bracelet. The point is: sometimes you need to turn a negative situation into a positive by giving yourself a congratulatory gift instead of just paying bills with a commission check. It's important to reward yourself.

KEEPING IT TOGETHER

When transactions start falling apart, we need to use both our negotiation skills and our people skills to hold things together. Ultimately, it will be up to us to resell a house we listed or find another house for a buyer.

First and foremost, we need to put the client's feelings above our own. Try to uncover any underlying agendas that may have caused a transaction to fall apart. Then, give your client permission to walk away, if that's what's best for them.

Your client is mourning a loss as well. They may have put a lot of emotional energy, time, and money into this process with nothing to show for it. Explain the process to them. If it's a buyer, give them space to mourn before moving forward to sell them another house. If it's a seller, re-list the house ASAP, of course. Take this opportunity to revisit their original motivation to move.

If you have a good relationship with your client, you will eventually make the sale. In the meantime, revisit what you have to be grateful for. Knowing that I can return to my own beautiful home grounds me. I know if I do all of the right things I will be rewarded financially in the end.

BE A CONSULTANT, NOT A SOCIAL WORKER

I approach my role as a realtor more like a consultant than a salesperson. I know I am the best person to guide my clients through this stressful journey, and I love connecting very deeply with people.

Making the decision to move is often more about emotions and underlying agendas than it is about logistics. I like to look into someone's eyes and reach into their soul to find out what is truly going on in their life.

Realtors help people through pivotal points in their lives as they transition from one place into another. There are many motivators that drive people to move: the loss of a spouse; a job opportunity; a growing family; an empty nest; or simply the joy of wanting live in a better, or different, environment. We need to be sensitive to all of these situations and respond accordingly.

They say that death, divorce, and buying or selling a house are the most stressful events in a person's life—in that order. While realtors deal with the details of these transactions every day, we forget that most people do this less than a handful of times in their lives. A seller may be very emotionally attached to their home, and find it particularly hard to let go.

We are here to guide them through this process, and alleviate as much stress as possible. While it is important to support our clients, try to focus on being empathetic versus sympathetic. Think of it this way: oncologists are empathetic. Their role is to evaluate a patient's symptoms, identify their disease, and prescribe the best course of action. Physicians cannot be so sympathetic that their hearts break with each diagnosis.

I have seen, and coached, agents who behave more like social workers than realtors. Some of them even pay for home improvements when a client says they don't have enough money to make repairs or do upgrades to prepare for sale.

This is not necessarily a bad thing if an upgrade will add significant value and equity to a house. However, the homeowner should explore other avenues first. Perhaps a home equity loan would be a better option. They could also consider deferring payments to a contractor, or borrowing money from someone.

Don't be the first to volunteer to pay for a client's upgrades. It is not your house! Here's the barometer: It's got to be more important to them than it is to you. If you find yourself in the position of being the last resort, then protect yourself by securing a loan with either a lien on the house or some other legally binding contract.

I've also seen realtors get so caught up in a client's drama that they start sending them food, cleaning their homes and grocery shopping for them. Don't get me wrong, I am not against being a charitable human being and helping someone out on occasion. However, I see this becoming a habit for some agents, who feel this is part of their job description.

Perhaps helping clients at this level makes some realtors feel more valuable, or more needed. I think it takes away from their professionalism. You can choose to run your business like a social worker if it feeds another part of your soul. I am here to remind you that you are a realtor, a business person, and this is not part of your job description

As a professional realtor, you want your clients to respect you as an expert. Think about going to a doctor who is wavering on a diagnosis, but offers to pick up your medication because you're too sick to do it. Who would you trust more: the unsure, kind-hearted physician, or a more experienced doctor who says he has seen these symptoms many times before and knows exactly how to treat you? An experienced professional, with boundaries, conveys confidence. That is what you are striving for.

GET AHEAD OF GHOSTING

Sometimes a client relationship can go south before you even get started. We've all been ghosted. There's nothing more frustrating than taking buyers out on a Saturday or Sunday, spending a few hours looking at houses, joking and bonding, and then never hearing from them again.

I don't know why this happens. I can only imagine something changed their mind about the area, the process, or even buying a house right now. Perhaps they decided to wait awhile and are too embarrassed to tell you because they think they wasted your time.

This is why I like to be up front and give buyers "permission" to not buy now, or to not buy in my area. If this isn't the right town for them, I will happily refer them to a realtor in another area they're considering.

When you let people know you are OK with whatever they decide, you build trust because you're acting more like a consultant than a salesperson. This gives them space to be more honest with you, and with themselves.

Orly Steinberg "Only Orly"

MAKE TIME FOR YOU

Real estate is a seven days a week occupation. You are always working. Either you're getting ready for an appointment, you're on an appointment, you're working on a transaction, or you're working on your business. Realtors can be on call more than a doctor: answering questions, calming people down, and responding to leads.

Once in a while, you need to recharge your battery and take time off. Some realtors feel guilty about this. In some ways, that can be a good thing, because it means you have the drive and ambition to constantly be thinking about your business. However, it's also important to know when to shut down and take some time off.

When you are off, give yourself permission to truly be off. Act like you're in a movie theater: turn your phone off and focus on something other than work. Nothing bad will happen. I promise you.

You are not a brain surgeon, and no one is going to die on the operating room table if you don't answer the phone right away. The caller will leave you a voice mail message, email, or text you, and you can get back to them when you're ready.

This will give you time to think about your response and offer a solution. It's better to respond proactively, instead of reacting to someone venting at you as soon as you pick up the phone.

No one wants to feel like a deer caught in the headlights. If you know what someone wants, you can think about their question, or their problem, and get back to them with a resolution.

SET BOUNDARIES

Many years ago, when I was pregnant with Jaymee and on bedrest, I was forced to set boundaries. First, I made a commitment not to answer phones after 7 pm. Realtors are notorious for communicating with each other, and their clients, until 11 pm or later, thinking this is what they have to do.

In fact, realtors are the biggest abusers of each other's time. It's more about ego than anything else. Trust me, as I mentioned before, no one will die on an operating room table if you don't talk to someone about a transaction after 7 pm. Your doctors, attorneys and accountants won't call you after 7 pm unless it's an emergency. Your obligation ends there, too.

This doesn't mean I won't listen to voicemail, read texts, or answer emails. But I only respond if something is truly important; and 90% of the late night communications can wait until morning. I've even had realtors call me at 10 pm to ask me for feedback on a listing or confirm inspections. We have business hours for a reason.

A realtor's input is not that crucial that we need to respond right away at all hours. It's not a life or death situation. Even if a deal is falling apart, sometimes it's important to sleep on it.

Most people are just reaching out to get something off their plate before they go to bed. They don't necessarily want to engage. Even if they do, it can wait until tomorrow. I recognize this is a choice and a discipline. It's very hard for most realtors not to respond after 7 pm; however, I choose to use this time for me and my family.

MAKE THE MOST OF YOUR TIME

You'll feel better about taking time off to recharge when you know you've done everything you can to grow your business. It takes self-discipline to prioritize and focus on the things you want, and need, to do to achieve your goals.

It is so easy to get distracted from doing "dollar productive activities". If you are not prospecting, showing houses, and negotiating, you are not being dollar productive. These are the only things that will put dollars in your pocket. Everything else is busy work.

Always be prepared, and have at least 10 pre-list packets and buyer consultation packets ready at any given time. I live by the motto: "Do today what you may not be able to do tomorrow." You never know how you will wake up the next day, or what could happen in the world to alter your plans.

I'm not saying you shouldn't do all of the other essential work you need to do to run your business. It's all necessary; however, the primary, most important tasks, are the ones I mentioned above. Block time for prospecting calls. Put listing and buyer appointments in your calendar, and work around them to schedule everything else.

Include at least an hour or two a week to work ON your business instead of IN your business:

- Give yourself time to pick up the notes you wrote at the last conference, and decide what you'd like to implement next.
- Review your P&L statement.
- Log the appointments you went on last month so you can track your success.
- Work on social media and marketing your business.

Chapter 14
Make Things Happen; Focus on Your Strengths

Are you reactive or proactive?

Most people live reactively, going about their daily lives reacting to whatever comes their way. I prefer a more proactive lifestyle.

Motivational speaker and author, Earl Nightingale, said if you want to be a success in life, watch what everyone else is doing and do the opposite. When they Zig...you Zag. I have taken that concept to heart.

I believe it's up to me to decide what my day will look like, and how I approach the inevitable challenges that lie ahead. I choose to live life by my own design, and react with a positive attitude. This takes work.

First, make a list of what you're good at, and acknowledge your own unique skill set. Multiple studies have shown the benefits of focusing on strengths, and how to expand them, instead of concentrating on improving weaknesses.

For example, I'm terrible at math and am not ashamed to admit it. However, I'm great at delegating. So if I need to figure out percentages or calculate challenging equations, I ask someone else to do it for me. Leading with strength is all about surrounding yourself with people who have different skill sets, and finding other ways to compensate for potential weaknesses.

Successful people live by a different set of rules. They don't conform to the norm. At times, I like to think "conventional rules" are for other people. The most important thing is that what I am doing makes sense for me.

For instance, every time my company launches a new technology that is supposed to make our lives easier, I wait for others to work out the kinks before I embrace it. I often end up staying with what I have if it works better for me. I still use the original Top Producer contact management program from 1993 because it works for me. The lesson here: don't be afraid to make your own decisions, and don't be so eager to follow the pack.

ANCHOR YOUR VISION

Work on your mindset. Try to envision roots that spiral into the ground beneath you to help keep you stable and grounded. When I practice yoga, the tree pose helps me actually visualize those roots growing below me from the bottom of my feet, cementing me like an anchor throughout my day. So when something bad happens—like a deal falling apart or a complicated inspection issue cropping up unexpectedly—it may shake me up a bit but it won't topple me over.

There will be days when multiple deals fall apart, and every phone call seems to be just another, progressively bigger problem. There is nothing you can do about those days. Shake them off by nurturing yourself.

Have lunch or dinner with a friend or loved one. Revisit your gratitude journal and feel blessed that the couple who just broke up, and is no longer buying the house you're listing, is not you.

Scale back to the very basics of life to remind yourself how things could always be worse. For me, it goes something like this: I am not that couple. I am going home to a husband who loves me. I have a beautiful home, and a beautiful, supportive family. We are all healthy and life is good. Today is just a shitty day, and tomorrow will be so much better.

ADAPT YOUR ATTITUDE

One day, in January 2018, I was feeling down on my business as I drove 25 minutes to a listing appointment for a $179,000 short sale. I called my dear friend and fellow realtor, Paula Clark, to vent about how business was slow, inventory was low, and here I was driving to a less than stellar appointment.

The average price range in Paula's Bergen County market is $550,000 or better. I knew there was nothing she could do but just listen and let me vent. It helps to have a friend you can trust to be vulnerable and transparent with—someone who won't judge.

The very next day, I received a "come list me" call from a seller for a beautiful $670,000 house. This time, when I called Paula I started singing: "What a difference a day makes, 24 little hours…" I ended up listing and selling that house in a bidding war in two weeks.

Everything really can turn around the very next day. It all depends on your attitude, and how you approach both disappointments and opportunities. You can either spiral down or spiral up depending on your mindset. You can adjust and relax if you know that you are prepared for whatever comes your way.

It truly can be lonely at the top. I recognize that no one is really going to feel sorry for "Only Orly" when I'm having a shitty day. It is important to be able to vent, though, and surround yourself with a supportive tribe of people who will listen and understand.

Even some of your friends may offer sympathy while they are secretly saying "Yes! I'm so glad that happened to her and not me." Very few people will genuinely be supportive when you're down, especially if you project an aura of success. It's just human nature.

It's OK. This moment, and this feeling, too, shall pass, and you'll be stronger for it.

Chapter 15
Attitude is Contagious; Make Yours Worth Catching

Attitudes can be contagious. Is yours worth catching?

People can sense if you are a positive or a negative person. Whether you focus on abundance or scarcity, you wear your attitude like clothes. A negative attitude is like bad BO. It stinks, and everyone around you can smell it. Sometimes, you have to fake it till you make it. Smile! It's show time!

A study done more than 30 years ago tracked high school students based on their yearbook pictures. Years later, those with the biggest smiles—not necessarily the best grades—had more money and better relationships.

When you smile, you not only look better, you have a sprint in your walk and more energy in your voice. People want to be near you. They want to do business with you. They want what you have. Remember the scene in *When Harry Met Sally* when Sally fakes an orgasm in Katz's Deli and another woman says, "I'll have what she's having."? This should be the attitude you project all the time.

Shield and protect yourself from negative people. I choose not to engage with them or let them into my life. I seem to have an invisible force field that repels them. They instinctively know they cannot dump their negativity on me. Of course, I listen to friends when they have a problem, but I'm not interested in hearing about someone's perpetually negative drama.

I choose to surround myself with positive, uplifting people. It's called "sacred selfishness." It's all right to be "selfish" in order to protect yourself. This is a healthy practice.

This is not always possible when you need to engage with clients or co-workers who can be negative. In those cases, I have a filter system. I only engage with these negative people when it is necessary. I try to remain upbeat, send them my positive energy, smile, and move on.

MAKING CHOICES

I believe we wake up every morning with choices. Those choices are often based on our belief systems and core values. We make a choice to either wake up earlier in order to work out and get more done, or sleep a bit longer because we feel our body needs more rest. Or maybe we just feel like staying in bed. And that's OK, too.

Long ago, I chose to have a good life. I made a very conscious decision in my early 20s to pursue a life filled with good friends, a fulfilling job I enjoy, and authentic, loving relationships. I knew I would have to work at creating a life full of luxury, comforts, and fun that includes travel, culture and the arts.

I chose to surround myself with positive like-minded people who would inspire and motivate me to be the best person I could be both professionally and personally. I chose to shield myself from negative people who didn't share the same core values and would bring me down.

DEFINING ABUNDANCE AND SCARCITY; A REAL-LIFE COMPARISON

As I read more and more books, went to numerous conferences, invested in coaching, and then chose to coach others, I saw how some people choose a life of abundance, while others live a life of scarcity.

A person with an abundance mindset believes there is always more of everything in life, whether it's money, relationships, resources, or opportunities. Alternatively, someone with a scarcity mentality always lives in fear that they are going to lose their time or money.

A scarcity minded person always sees the glass half empty. They are always expecting something to go wrong. When something is going right, they are sure it is just temporary. This good fortune will surely not last, and things are bound to go wrong again. It's almost as if they are more comfortable with scarcity. They seem to be afraid of abundance, because they'll be disappointed when it doesn't last.

How do you choose to approach life? Realtors deal with challenges and disappointments every week—oftentimes daily. In scarcity mode, these challenges can drown you and set you on a negative spiral, where one thing after another starts going wrong. In abundance mode, you are more apt to look for opportunities to grow and learn from difficult situations.

Winston Churchill defines success as "the ability to move from failure to failure without losing your enthusiasm." It has been proven time and time again that mindset can radically affect the course of your life. Overwhelming research shows the way you think about yourself and the world around you can drastically change the way you learn, how you handle stress, how you generate success, your resiliency, and even how your immune system functions.

I have such an over active sense of abundance that I even think I can will the weather to turn into a warm sun shiny day when I am planning an event or a party.

Chapter 16
Adapting through Crisis; And Crises Will Happen

"Circumstances do not make the man or woman, they merely reveal them."

—Brian Tracy

Anything unsustainable can, and most likely will, collapse during a crisis. However, when systems collapse, people rise up. A crisis provides opportunities to re-evaluate and make your business, and your personal life, more sustainable.

We have all had, or will have, crises and adversity in our lives. These crises often make a strong impact on our lives, emotions, finances, and businesses.

I have already been through a few down markets, which reinforce the need to plan for financial uncertainty. I had a double mastectomy, which left me unable to work for more than two months, and I quarantined with my family during the COVID-19 virus, which put a pause button on the entire world.

A realtor's income stream is unreliable at best. When the mortgage market falls, like it did in 2008, we learn, firsthand, how important it is to not over leverage ourselves. Having cash reserves is critical. That's why I always stress putting away 25% of every commission check as if it was a referral fee to yourself.

Those of us who take that lesson to heart end up more financially secure, with more equity, so that when the next wave hits we are in much better shape to hold tight and capitalize on opportunities when the market takes off again. COVID-19 is a perfect example of this. For months, the market came to a halt as people remained in a virtual lockdown. Realtors who were prepared to wait out the lull were rewarded when houses in the suburbs became a hot commodity for people who no longer had to show up for their jobs in the city.

Maintaining the right mindset while working through a crisis is critical. It's hard to remain positive when there is so much uncertainty. Your routines become a lifeline. My morning ritual, for example, which includes allotting time for my gratitude journal, affirmations, and physical exercise, has kept me grounded through many ups and downs.

Pay attention to your business routines, too. What daily tasks help you stay productive and move your business forward while working through challenges? Look for holes and weaknesses, too. What is holding up well? What isn't? What cracks in the foundation need to be shored up?

EMBRACE CHANGE

"If we don't change, we don't grow. If we don't grow, we are not really living. Growth demands a temporary surrender of security."

—Gail Sheehy

Success comes to those who can adapt to change and get in front of the inevitable. Stay in curiosity mode, instead of giving in to fear. Learn to do business differently. Implement new systems that will make your business stronger.

Find out what your superpower is, and what sustains you. Make small tweaks in your routine where necessary, re-evaluate your finances, and explore new options for personal growth. If you are worried that a new approach might fail, consider the worst case scenario. Can you live with it? If so, then go for it!

Figure out what you can control, and learn how to deal with what you cannot. During the COVID-19 quarantine, many of us learned how to work from home for the first time. We had to figure out how to share space with family members, who were also adapting to their "new normal." We picked up new skills out of necessity: mastering Zoom meetings with co-workers and clients; creating virtual showings; and relying on digital transactions for closings and other important documentation. In many cases, we discovered we preferred some of these new approaches as ways to expedite the way we do business.

Give yourself permission to relax and do things you enjoy. We all need distractions sometimes to recharge, refocus, and just have fun.

Give yourself permission to lose it, too, when the stress gets to be too much. It's OK; just don't wallow in it for too long. Do a mindset reset and get ready to start tackling what needs to be done.

Pick one area of your life and take steps to move forward. If it's your health, choose one thing you can do differently or better. Add one more exercise to your day. Make better eating choices: cut out sugar, or add more vegetables.

If you decide to focus on your business, try doing one thing a day that makes you feel productive and moves your business forward. Commit to calling 10 past clients. Do a Facebook live post or video.

Just committing to one thing every day can help you feel good about yourself and move you forward when you feel paralyzed. This is crucial for your emotional well-being.

PREPARE FOR THE NEXT CRISIS

Before you settle into a more normal flow again, put an action plan together for the next time "shit happens". When things are going well, it's easy to become complacent. We don't want to think about the next crisis while we're busy getting back to enjoying life; however, that is the best time to review what just happened and come up with different ways to handle things next time.

There are so many lessons to be learned during a crisis, and opportunities for personal growth as you reflect on your character and the character of those around you. Take the time to recognize both your strengths and frailties. What strengths can you now tap in to on a regular basis? Who can you turn to for help to support your weaknesses? If you don't have a support system already, start building one. I guarantee you will need it at some point in your life.

At times like these, I rely on my 5 Pillars to make sure I am maintaining a strong foundation. The most important thing is health. We need to feel good, and strong in our bodies, in order to have a healthy mindset. Your morning routine, which includes exercise, sets the tone for the day.

Relationships are important, too. Reach out to the positive people in your life who energize you, and minimize contact with energy vampires. Connect with your support people regularly so you can lift each other up when necessary. Sharing your vulnerability gives people permission to be vulnerable, too, and helps deepen relationships with people who matter most.

During the COVID-19 shut down, we realized how important it was to connect with others as we embraced Zoom and other technologies that allowed us to see and hear each other, even if we couldn't be together in the same location. Because of the pandemic, we are now more comfortable both socializing and doing business in a digital world.

Out of necessity, we reached outside of our comfort zones to do many more things virtually: classes, meetings, conferences, religious services, doctor appointments... The list goes on. As we move forward, I envision even more technologies emerging that will make it easier to do business with buyers and sellers who aren't able to meet with you in person.

EMERGE STRONGER

During the COVID-19 pandemic, I learned how to facilitate Real Estate Mastermind sessions, which is now one of my super powers. I had always wanted to do this, and was scheduled to take a class in Ohio to learn how when we were ordered to shelter at home. The in-person certification class turned into a three-day Zoom class, which was ideal because it taught me how to do Masterminds with Zoom.

This could not have come at a more opportune time. I have now led several of these virtual classes, which I would not have known how to do if not for COVID-19.

Although I had been technologically challenged, I used this time to embrace this new world, and move my life and business forward by doing market evaluations online, conducting a "downsizing" seminar online, and leading virtual Real Estate Mastermind sessions.

Orly Steinberg "Only Orly"

Try to look for the blessings that come from adversity. Sometimes we see them in the moment, and sometimes they appear in the rear view mirror. The important thing is to be open to receiving and growing from them.

Who do you want to be during, and after, a crisis?

I have found that I tend to be more compassionate, more empathetic, and more aware of others. I want to serve my community, and help wherever I can. I look for posts on Facebook that identify needs, gather donations for foodbanks, or find other urgent causes. I use my social media platforms to provide my community with positive, valuable information.

Staying focused on my daily intentions and affirmations helps me stay grounded and move forward so that I can grow and learn from every situation. It's about choosing who I want to be in the moment. It's about finding my purpose, which is to be a positive beacon of light that shines both for myself and for others. It's about being mindful of my own emotions as well as those of people around me.

WHO DO YOU CHOOSE TO BE IN A CRISIS?

When have you had to overcome adversity?

_____

_____

How did you get through the crisis?

_____

_____

What strengths did you discover?

_____

_____

What super powers did you develop?

_____

_____

_____

What can you do in your community to make an impact?

_____

_____

_____

FINANCIAL ADVERSITY —
AND THE IMPORTANCE OF YOUR CREDIT SCORE

Struggling with adversity can affect your credit score. When the market tanked in the last quarter of 2008, we were all paralyzed, knowing that everything was going to change. We held our breaths, waiting for a sign of what was to come.

What came was a deluge of homes hitting the market that were upside down on their mortgages, with no way out but short sales or foreclosures. This truly opened my eyes. So many people were so financially unstable that they were hanging by a thread due to bad choices, a bad market, and other life issues that seemed to collide in a perfect storm.

By 2010, I started counseling sellers like a social worker, trying to help them figure out the best course of action for each scenario. If I asked the right questions over the phone, I could decide before I even left the office who was salvageable and who wasn't. I felt like an ER triage doctor.

The answers to these questions revealed a lot:

- Why are you selling?
- Where are you going?
- When did you buy your house?
- How much do you currently owe on the mortgage?
- If you are upside down on your mortgage, what is your game plan, if you have one?

I started playing a game. When I entered a home, I would evaluate its condition in order to guess the homeowner's credit score. I observed that a person's values tend to be congruent with how they live their life.

There is no way a messy, dirty house with dirty laundry everywhere, and dishes in the sink, could equal a credit score of more than 690. Sellers who were neat and clean, and had all the appropriate documentation ready for me on the kitchen table, clearly had a credit score over 700. The few exceptions were sellers who had been blindsided by losing a job, divorce, or medical issues and bills.

I advised my three daughters to make sure they knew the credit score of anyone they dated seriously, let alone married. At first, I was half joking; then I realized I wasn't. It is important to know the core financial values of someone who you are going to live with or marry.

Would you want to be surprised that someone close to you had huge debt, lived above their means, or just didn't pay their bills? Would you want to inherit those issues? I think not.

I am proud to say that all of my daughters are now married, or in serious relationships with men who have credit scores in the high 700s.

WHAT DOES YOUR CREDIT SCORE SAY ABOUT YOU?

Do you know your credit score?

_____

_____

_____

Is your credit score congruent with your lifestyle?

_____

_____

_____

What changes do you need to make to increase your credit score, so that it aligns with your core values?

_____

_____

_____

_____

How can you prepare to minimize damages to your credit score during adverse times?

_____

_____

_____

Chapter 17
Living the Legacy; Charting Your Future

"Twenty years from now, you will be more disappointed by the things you didn't do than by the ones you did do. So throw off the bowlines, sail away from the safe harbor, and catch the trade wind in your sails. Explore, Dream, Discover."

—Author Unknown

What drives you? Is it wealth? If so, for what purpose? Is it ego? Do you just want to have more things, or maybe a few specific things?

Think about it: everyone wants more money. We're all chasing the dollar at some level. Every seminar I have ever gone to tells you how to work smarter, and harder, in order to get to the next level.

I built my career, and my life, on many of the principles I learned at these conferences and seminars. I have spoken, and led educational sessions, at many of them, too, from Star Power, to CRS (Certified Residential Specialist) and REV (Real Estate Vision).

These are all wonderful places to learn how to build your brand and your business. However, the question in the back of my mind was always: "At what cost?" Later, I started asking myself: "How much is enough?"

I watched the toll this constant drive took on realtors I knew, and saw how it led to divorces and severed relationships with family members. They were too caught up in appearances, and what they thought their lifestyle should be like. They were building wealth and living beyond their means, only to have everything crash around them when the market spiraled downward.

As I became more successful, I, too, started feeling like my entire identity was about "being a realtor." I needed to be the best realtor I could be—nothing less than perfect. I was so proud of this identity, and I carried myself proudly. It's a wonderful feeling to know that you have "arrived," and that you are accomplished, and recognized, in your field.

And then I started to ask myself: "Who are you? Really?" If I wasn't a realtor, how would I identify myself? It was becoming hard to separate myself from that identity. It was so easy, and comforting, to just be "that successful realtor". However, I knew at a core level that it wasn't enough, and it would not sustain me in the future when I was no longer working in real estate.

I started to think about retirement. Who would I be then? What would be my legacy? Peeling off the layers of my identity, piece by piece, I realized my true legacy was right in front of me. It is the family I created with my husband, Aharon, and our three daughters. In a world marred with divorce and dysfunctional homes, we raised three amazing, wonderful women while keeping our relationship thriving and loving.

My legacy is also the multitude of people in my life who love and respect me. It is the friends who seek my wisdom, love and joy of living. My legacy is my tribe. It is critical to find people who understand you, who get you, who accept you, and who make you feel like you belong. These are the people who lift you up, just as much as you lift them. Without your tribe, it's easy to get lost. We truly sustain each other.

Chapter 18
In Conclusion; Baby Steps...

"The greatest discovery of my generation is that a human being can alter his life by altering his attitude of mind."

—William James

I realize that after reading this book you might feel a bit overwhelmed. It's a lot to take in, and it takes small baby steps to implement. It is very challenging to put all of these practices into action all at once. It's like the saying goes: "How do you eat an elephant? One bite at a time."

We've talked about money. We've talked about how to run your real estate business profitably and efficiently. We've talked about making and meeting financial goals.

We've talked about making time, reserving energy, and setting aside money for the rest of the things that make life full and worthwhile.

It's not realistic to read this book once and expect to be able to start doing everything I've done to achieve balance in my life. It took me years to come up with the right approach, and the right formula, for me.

Start with the Wheel of Life and focus on your 5 Pillars. Address your weakest link and build from there. Re-read the chapters you want to focus on. I suggest you pick one aspect a month. Identify a few things you can implement now and throughout the year.

Then come back, reassess, keep doing things that are working, make a few tweaks if necessary, and add a few more.

Ultimately, achieving balance, and enjoying a full life, is all about mindset. Choose a positive attitude. Choose joy. Live life with love and abundance each and every day—whatever that means for you.

If you'd like to delve deeper into any aspect I've introduced in this book, I have included my personal reading list. I hope you gain as much from these resources as I have.

Please reach out to me and share any new resources you discover as well. I'm also available for coaching, speaking, and Real Estate Masterminds. You can reach me at orly@onlyorly.com or go to my website: www.mindsetresetforrealestatesuccess.com.

My Reading List

"Your living is determined not so much by what life brings you as by the attitude you bring to life; not so much by what happens to you, as by the way your mind looks at what happens."

—Lewis L. Dunnington

I am a voracious reader, always learning, and adapting what I learn to how I approach life. Here is a list of books that have guided me. I have introduced you to key concepts from many of them in my writing. Here is a chance for you to dig deeper. I hope you will gain as much from them as I have.

Please reach out to me and share any new resources you discover as well. You can reach me at Orly@onlyorly.com.

Noteworthy thoughts:

- Whenever I read a book, I like to truly dive in with gusto and get as much out of it as I can. So go ahead, dig in, highlight passages that speak to you, and make notes. I hope you will do that with this book as well.

- I often download a book on Audible so I can listen to it while I'm on the treadmill or driving, and then I buy a hard copy so I can re-read it, highlight references, implement tactics, and share information.

A FEW OF MY FAVORITES:

(7L) The Seven Levels of Communication: Go from Relationships to Referrals
—Michael J Maher

MONEY Master the Game: 7 Simple Steps to Financial Freedom
—Tony Robbins

Awaken the Giant Within: How to Take Immediate Control of Your Mental, Emotional, Physical and Financial Destiny
—Tony Robbins

Ninja Selling: Subtle skills. Big Results
—Larry Kendall

Take the Stairs: 7 Steps to Achieving True Success
—Rory Vaden

Profit First: Transform Your Business from a Cash-Eating Monster to a Money-Making Machine
—Mike Michalowicz

Black Belt of the Mind: A Conscious Approach to Wealth
—Dr. Fred Grosse

Millionaire Success Habits: The Gateway to Wealth & Prosperity
—Dean Graziosi

Good to Great: Why Some Companies Make the Leap...And Others Don't
—Jim Collins

The One Minute Manager Balances Work and Life
—Ken Blanchard

15 Invaluable Laws of Growth
—John C. Maxwell

Developing the Leader Within You
—John C. Maxwell

The Leadership Handbook: 26 Critical Lessons Every Leader Needs
—John C. Maxwell

No Limits: Blow the CAP Off Your Capacity
—John C. Maxwell

The 17 Indisputable Laws of Teamwork: Embrace Them and Empower Your Team
—John C. Maxwell

Intentional Living: Choosing a Life That Matters
—John C. Maxwell

SHIFT: How Top Real Estate Agents Tackle Tough Times
—Gary Keller

The ONE Thing: The Surprisingly Simple Truth Behind Extraordinary Results
—Gary Keller

The Millionaire Real Estate Agent
—Gary Keller

Raving Fans: A Revolutionary Approach to Customer Service
—Ken Blanchard and Sheldon Bowles

As You Wish
—Carol Gates and Tina Shearon

One Word That Will Change Your Life
—John Gordon, Dan Britton, and Jimmy Page

Rich Dad Poor Dad
—Robert T. Kiyosaki

Who Moved My Cheese?
—Dr. Spencer Johnson

First Things First
—Stephen Covey

The 7 Habits of Highly Effective People
—Stephen Covey

Principle Centered Leadership
—Stephen Covey

6 Steps to 7 Figures: A Real Estate Professional's Guide to Building Wealth and Creating Your Own Destiny
—Pat Hiban

The Energy Bus: 10 Rules to Fuel Your Life, Work, and Team with Positive Energy
—Jon Gordon

The Platinum Rule: Discover the Four Basic Business Personalities and How They Can Lead You to Success
—Tony Alessandra PHD and Michael J. O'Connor PhD

You are a Badass: How to Stop Doubting Your Greatness and Start Living an Awesome Life
—Jen Sincero

About the Author

photo credit - Melissa Griegel Photography

Orly Steinberg is a top selling realtor, speaker, coach and team builder. She and her husband, Aharon, live in a wooded suburb of New Jersey, where they raised their three daughters, Tara, Monica, and Jaymee. Along the way, she and her "Only Orly" team built a real estate business that is ranked #1 locally, and in the top 1% nationally. She is now building a speaking and coaching network for sharing her mindset reset for earning, and enjoying, success while cultivating a balanced life.

Made in the USA
Coppell, TX
26 July 2021